PASSPORT TO THE BIBLE

R.P. Hromas

LIVING STUDIES
Tyndale House
Publishers, Inc.
Wheaton, Illinois

First printing, Living Studies edition, November 1983
Library of Congress Catalog Card Number 83-50013
ISBN 0-8423-4802-6

Printed in the United States of America

CONTENTS

YOU CAN! HERE'S HOW!

You can! That's the greatest word of encouragement I can give you today as you begin to see the Bible as a *practical* book, totally applicable to your personal everyday life.

You can . . .

. . . understand the Bible for yourself.

. . . use the Bible to answer your questions in life, great or small.

. . . find Bible-based solutions to the problems in your life.

You can . . .

. . . find peace of mind.

. . . experience fulfillment in your life as never before.

. . . know the deep joy of those who love the Lord and live by the eternal principles expressed in the Bible.

You can . . .

. . . make the Bible come alive in and give life to your everyday walk on earth.

This book deals with *how* that can happen for you.

The Bible is a book about people. It tells the experiences of people who have trusted in God, people just like you and me.

The Bible is a book of prophecies that have become history. It is also a book of prophecies still to be fulfilled, many of which will be fulfilled in your lifetime. These prophecies relate to *people.*

The Bible is a book of illustrations that tells how ordinary *people* can live their lives in total harmony with God. These are practical pointers to help individuals make it through each day on earth.

The Bible is a book about and for all people . . . including you! God's greatest desire is that you understand his love for you and know his Word, that you might have eternal life. All of the Bible is given to you to enable you to know God.

The way in which we come to a full understanding of God and our relationship with him is *progressive.*

When we stop to think about it, we see that our lives are progressive in a number of ways.

We learn to walk before we run,
Paddle around in shallow pools before we enter deep waters,
Eat baby food before we tackle T-bone steaks,
Learn our ABC's before we read the classics.

Indeed, no area of our lives escapes this law of progression. We often call the process *growth.* In some instances, we might call it depth—a deepening of our understanding about a person, issue, or process.

Our approach to the Bible must follow this same universal principle. An understanding of the Bible comes

line by line,
day by day,
experience by experience,
passage by passage,
application by application.

We experience an ever-growing and ever-deepening understanding of and appreciation for the eternal truth of God as we read the Bible over a period of time.

And what a magnificent book the Bible is! No matter how many times we may read a passage, we find new insights or new ways to apply God's Word to our daily lives. It's almost as if the meaning of the Bible is in layers—with rich meaning on the surface for those just beginning to read the Bible, and richer and richer meaning for those who read the Bible more often and study it more diligently. We will never reach a *perfect* understanding of the Bible on earth, but the constant pursuit of understanding can fill our daily lives to overflowing with purpose and joy.

This book is also arranged in a progressive manner. Each chapter spills into the next, encouraging you to grow . . . and grow some more. *Put this book to work!*

DO YOU KNOW THE AUTHOR OF THE BIBLE?

Knowing the author of the Bible is the most important thing in life. His name is Jesus. The Bible tells us about him. It tells us he is the Son of God. He died for our sins, was resurrected, and is alive today. It also tells us that he was *the Word made flesh.* He existed before the world was created. His life and the words of the Bible exist in perfect harmony; they are one message.

The wonderful thing about Jesus is that we *can know him personally.* He became flesh—a human being—so we could totally understand him and he us. We are born with spirit, soul, and body—just as he was.

The first step in knowing Jesus is to invite him to share your life—to come into your life and to cleanse any area that is displeasing to him. Part of that invitation must be a commitment to develop a relationship with God: to follow his Word, to talk with him, obey him, and serve him, and to receive from him the blessings and benefits he has for you. When your spirit is united with God's Holy Spirit, then you are in a position to know God and he is in a position to help you. Your human spirit and his Holy Spirit mesh together like gears in a great mechanism.

I have a neighbor who knows a former president of the United States. They visit in each other's homes. I've met him briefly. I've read his books. I know people who know him. But I don't know him personally. He doesn't stay at my house or eat meals with me.

You can know people who know God—who walk and talk with him daily. You can meet Jesus briefly at church. You may have read what Jesus has written. A *relationship* with Jesus, however, is one in which he lives with you all the time—he is invited into every area of your life. This is *knowing* Jesus.

Let me put it another way. Suppose I have an apple—a nice, ripe, juicy one. Can you hear the crunch in your mind's ear as I bite into my apple? It's just crunchy enough to make a snap between my teeth. It isn't mealy; the skin isn't bitter. I find that my hunger is satisfied as I eat my crisp, cool apple. On a different level, I'm satisfied and glad that I'm not eating something that will give me a brief sugar high. I'm eating something truly nourishing to every cell of my body.

Now I can tell you all of this, even to the point of having your mouth water, but *my* apple isn't going to do *you* a bit of good. Until you take a bite of your own apple and experience it and allow it to nourish your life, you really can't know what eating an apple is all about! The same is true with Jesus. You must *know* him for yourself in a personal way. The Bible says in Psalm 34:8 that we are to taste and see that the Lord is good.

Knowing Jesus is no light matter. This is the most serious, awesome relationship you'll ever develop. It requires responsibility and commitment.

The key to commitment is making a decision. You have to *decide* to invite Jesus to participate with you in every circumstance and every experience of your life. You have to *decide* to read the Bible. Those two decisions must go hand in hand. Otherwise, your reading of the Bible will be an empty experience for you. Equally true, without Bible reading your relationship with Jesus won't grow.

You may ask, "Why is it essential to know Jesus in order to understand the Bible? Why can't I make sense of the Bible without a personal relationship with its author?"

Because the Bible is a spiritual book, the only truly spiritual book on earth. The Bible clearly says that only two things on earth are eternal: God's Word and persons who have accepted God into their lives. The reason these things are eternal is this: God's Spirit dwells within both. If you have invited Jesus into your life, you have his Spirit within you. You have the promise of eternal life.

The Bible too is endued with God's Spirit. The real meaning and message of the Bible lies beyond the mere black and white marks on the paper. Your mind may understand the words, but unless your *spirit* also embraces them you are missing the full message of the Bible. The Bible is filled with God's Spirit, and it can only be thoroughly understood by readers who are also filled with God's Spirit. Knowing Jesus personally makes it possible for you to relate to the Bible on spiritual terms.

So, I ask you now at the beginning of our sharing in this book . . .

Have you decided to unite your life with Jesus?
Have you decided to unite your spirit with the Holy Spirit?
Have you decided to make an earnest attempt to understand the Bible and to read it daily?
Have you decided to live according to what the Bible says?

If not, I invite you to make those decisions. I invite you to ask Jesus to come into your life and live there forever. If you have never talked to Jesus, you may have some questions about all this. Actually, it's like meeting a person for the first time. You're never sure just how to talk to a stranger, right? But the solution to the problem is really quite simple in both cases: start talking. Speak out loud. Say a sentence or two to Jesus. Ask him to come into your life and to be the Lord of your life—to rule every area of your life and to cleanse all those areas that cause you guilt, anxiety, and fear.

The Lord Jesus will look beyond your words to your intentions, your will, and to the meaning you give to your words. He will look at your sincerity and at your true desire to turn away from your past and to *know* him. When anyone calls out to Jesus with this deep, sincere desire, he always responds. That's his promise to you.

When you know the author of a book, it's always more exciting to read the book! This is true of the Bible. When you *know* Jesus—and have a personal relationship with him—you'll want to find out all you can about him. You'll want to find out what he can do to transform your life and help you to live an abundant, full, joyful life. You'll *want* to read the Bible, and here's the way I suggest you begin . . .

BOOK I

GETTING INTO THE BIBLE— FIVE MINUTES A DAY

"Will you give five minutes a day for peace of mind?"

My new acquaintance and I were standing in a carwash in California. We had experienced an earthquake that morning, and it had caused quite a bit of damage. Everybody, it seemed, was more interested than usual in knowing what the Bible says and about how to establish a relationship with God. If Jesus was the answer, they surely wanted to know him . . . *that* morning anyway. What had started out to be a simple trip to the carwash had turned into a great opportunity to talk about God.

This man was honest with himself and with me in his reply. "I've always wanted to know God, and I'm willing to try anything, but I don't think I can make religion work in my life. I know my weaknesses and the demands of my profession, and I don't think I can come through for God."

He was a troubled man, especially troubled at that time in his relationship with his wife. He had tried many avenues in his search for peace of mind. I asked him again, "Would you give five minutes a day for peace of mind?"

"What do I have to do?" he asked.

"Read your Bible five minutes a day."

"Is that all?"

"No. First, I'd like for you to pray this simple prayer with me:

Lord Jesus, if you are real—if you exist—I want to know you. So I invite you to be a part of my life. Take away anything about me that you don't like. And when I read your Book, cause me to understand it and apply it to my life. I will make an effort to love and serve you. In Jesus' name I pray. Amen."

This man prayed with me and decided to give Bible reading a try. His five minutes in the morning grew into five minutes both morning and evening. After about ten days, his wife began reading the Bible with him. They began to watch church programs on television and to listen to radio stations that broadcast spiritually uplifting music. These programs had seemed boring to them before, but now they seemed beautiful. Step by step their lives began to change. They realized they were living by new values. They approached their problems in a different manner. They might be in the middle of an argument—but come time for the husband to leave for work, they were faced with their pact to read the Bible together for a few minutes before he left. What a blow to an argument!

Jesus became central in their lives, and Bible reading became an important part of each day. The problems that were confusing their lives were smoothed over. The Word of God resulted in a marvelous transformation of their lives and their marriage. Beginning with just five minutes a day, this man and his wife *did* find peace of mind.

We have a friend who is a young married woman. She had trained for and reached the height of her career and by all standards of the world led a very successful life. She had married a college graduate with a successful business of his own, and they had a daughter who was beautiful and just right in every way. This friend began to think, Is this all there really is in life? She began to have anxiety attacks.

The attacks led her to seek out the best psychiatrists in the world. Eventually she was taking forty-two high-potency pills a day. She read books, talked to everyone she knew, and was loved and supported by her husband and mother. She had gone to church as a young girl, so she had heard about Jesus. But she didn't realize that he could be the complete answer for her life. The attacks grew worse, and she agreed to enter a private institution to see if that would help. She accepted Jesus as her personal Lord while she was a patient.

The morning she left the institution, she stopped by our weekly Bible study class en route to her home—still wearing her hospital armband. That morning she discovered that God's Word held the answers for putting her life back together. She went home and began to read her Bible—five minutes a day. Her hunger was great; her need was great.

When it came time to take the pills, she'd sit down and read the Bible for five minutes instead. From that morning to this day, she has not taken another tranquilizer! (This same method can apply to any temptation in life—food, alcohol, lust.)

The five minutes a day grew into longer study periods until she had read the Bible from cover to cover three times in six months. She read and read the Bible, even when she didn't understand every detail of every passage. She knew in her spirit that the Bible held the answer to her needs. She knew the reading of its truths would reprogram and mend her broken life with the absolutes of the universe. Today she is well in body, mind, and spirit. She leads the kind of life every wife and mother on earth longs to live.

It was this same search for answers that led me into Bible reading and study. When we married, my husband was in graduate school. Simply put, we didn't have much money. We were faced with my putting him through school, and I had many questions about life but not many answers. I had trusted God to supply money for my own schooling, and he had always supplied enough—in fact, a little extra so I could help others around me. But there I was, feeling alone in a marriage with difficult circumstances and wondering if I could make enough money and have enough strength to work and then come home and clean house and cook the kind of meals that would be nutritious for a man who had to study nearly twenty hours a day, in a town where I didn't know anybody or my way around. How was I ever going to have my soul restored enough to do that day after day after day? I knew from my parents' example that the Bible was the only place I could begin to find the answers. My mother, a widow from the time I was twelve, had raised her two children according to biblical principles. I knew that what had worked for her had to work for me. The Bible *had* to have the answers to my problems, and they had to be practical ones that could help me personally and daily.

I began to read—five minutes a day. I'd read the Bible in the ladies' room on lunch breaks or in the supermarket parking lot—taking advantage of every spare minute I could find. I read for longer periods whenever possible. That was the beginning.

The Bible showed me ways to select food and to cook. I found that the Bible also explains shortcuts for doing housework, ways to encourage a husband, and ideas for making money to supply our needs in everyday life! I literally lived by the Bible. It became our manual for life. And when our children came, the Bible became our manual for rearing them. The Bible never failed to provide the answers for us . . . and it doesn't fail today.

That's why, when people ask me, "Why study the Bible?" I answer with great confidence, "Because it can change your life!"

It's just that simple: the Bible changes lives.

The Bible is not a book of theory. It gives practical answers to everyday problems. In fact, there's not a problem in your life that's not matched by a solution in the Bible. You just need to know where to look. And when you find the answer, you need to receive it into your life and apply it in practical ways.

My husband is a scientist and a committed believer in the Bible. About twenty-five years ago I asked him, "Are we going to the moon?" At that time, many people were discussing whether we could and would put a man on the moon.

My husband said, "We already know *how* to go to the moon. It's all written—the theory is set. Now it's a matter of time and discipline and decisions. Those are the ingredients that will bring about a trip to the moon."

And that's where we are today in our trip through life. The Bible has the answers in black and white. The theory is just waiting for you to work it out in your life with time and discipline and decisions. Whatever your problem—from money to family difficulties with a spouse or children—the answer is in the Bible.

The secrets of the universe are there—about the stars and earth and about how to grow plants and work with the laws of nature.

- *The Bible tells us how to know God.*

We can experience God through the Holy Spirit in our hearts, but true understanding has to be built on a foundation of Bible truths.

- *The Bible tells us how to find eternal life.*

It tells us how to have our souls restored so our true personalities and identities can come shining through.

- *The Bible gives life to our inner person.*

It gives health to our bodies and tells us how to heal our inner persons.

It gives health to our souls and tells us how to heal broken relationships with others.

I don't know the answers to your life's questions, but I know where you can find the answers. Are you willing to look for them?

You may ask, "Where do I begin?" I invite you to make a commitment to read the Bible in this way:

First, read the Bible daily, five minutes a day. The truth of the Bible is like food for your soul. The Bible will literally become a part of you. The Bible says, "O taste and see that the Lord is good" (Psalm 34:8, KJV). This is what happens when you read the Bible.

Just as your body cannot live for very many days without food, so your spirit cannot go for very long without food to help it grow and develop. That's why it's important to read the Bible *daily.*

If you are just beginning to read the Bible regularly, you are like a newborn baby. Babies don't begin with five-course steak dinners. They begin with milk—small amounts regularly and often. This is the way to begin with Bible reading, too. That's why we say five minutes a day at first.

For awhile my husband and I kept horses, and once we lost a horse because it foundered from overeating. Horses need to be fed small amounts every day. It is the same for a new reader of the Word. Take the Bible as "sincere milk" (1 Peter 2:2, KJV). Look on your Bible reading as a *feeding* for your soul! Don't wait for an hour once a week.

You have no excuse for not finding five minutes a day, even with the busiest of schedules. You can always be five minutes late. You can lock yourself in the bathroom or sit in your car for five minutes. You can hide in your walk-in closet or stand at the kitchen sink for five minutes. You can find five minutes while waiting for a doctor, dentist, or beautician. You can always take a break for five minutes!

If you find that five minutes a day isn't enough to satisfy your hunger for the Word, try five minutes in the morning and five minutes in the evening for a few weeks. You must read enough Scripture so that it has a meaning for you. You must feel satisfied at the end of your feeding. This is the opposite of foundering. Too little food will leave you restless and hungry. You'll feel "flustrated" (my combination for feeling flustered and frustrated at the same time). Your soul will cry out like a baby that has its bottle taken away while she's still hungry.

You may need several five-minute feedings throughout the day. Your hunger may grow day by day. But don't miss a day. Be consistent in your spiritual feeding habits.

Second, read the Bible as if it were written only for you. Look for the personal application. Ask constantly, "How does this relate to me? How does this apply to me *today?*"

God knows the number of hairs on your head, and he desires to make his Word come alive to you in practical, personal ways.

I am *not* saying that you are the sole source of interpreting the Bible or that you can bend the Bible's message to fit your own life and your own ideas. Bible truths are eternal and absolute. The Bible spans all cultures, history, social levels, and occupations, all ages, races, and nationalities. But the way in which a particular passage of the Bible applies to your circumstances and your experience *is* unique to you each day.

Let me give you an example. You might be reading the Bible one day and come to a passage that tells you not to covet—not to be envious of the possessions of others. This is an eternal truth that is given to all people for all ages. But if you come across that passage of Scripture on a day when you are envious of a friend's position or wealth or new dress or fancy car, take it to heart. That's your kernel of truth, applicable to you right where you are! It's not only a *universal* law. It's God's Word to you for that day. Don't be jealous. (And who enjoys feeling jealousy anyway? It's to your advantage *not* to feel the energy-sapping tension of jealousy, and that's why God gave us that piece of advice.)

God's words are always for our benefit if we'll only accept them *personally.*

Mark it up! . . .

Don't be afraid to mark in your Bible. Your Bible is your personal property, waiting to be used as you use your other possessions. Many people seem to feel the Bible is too sacred to touch, much less scribble in. The *meaning* of the Bible *is* sacred. But the ink-on-parchment volume you hold is like a tool—it's to be used in personal, practical ways.

The same advice holds true for this book—mark it up! Circle, underline, or star passages that speak to you. Write in the margins. Fill the pages with *your* notes, anecdotes, ideas, and questions.

. . . and talk it up!

Don't be afraid to talk about the Bible. Ask friends questions about what puzzles you. Pray together with friends for insight into the Scriptures. Express your opinions. Pass on what God teaches you as you read. Share passages that seem to have a special impact on your life.

This way the Bible becomes more than personal, faith-building truth for you. It brings life to your *relationships* with others. It becomes a sturdy bridge between friends—a special bond that lasts for all eternity!

The truths of the Bible are like seeds. When they are planted in our hearts by reading and are watered by the inspiration and illumination of the Holy Spirit, they spring forth and grow in our actions and in our conversations. Our words and deeds mirror what we read.

Now let's deal with four very practical questions you may have.

1. "Where should I start reading?" I suggest the third chapter of the book of Matthew, the first book in the New Testament. The first chapter of Matthew is genealogy. It tells us the ancestry of Jesus. The second chapter is the Christmas story—but if it isn't the Christmas season or you aren't in the mood for that story, save it for Christmastime. The third chapter of Matthew gets you right into the words of Jesus, and that's the best place I know to start!

When you finish Matthew, I suggest you go to John—another Gospel with the same story, told from a different perspective and with a different emphasis. Then you may want to continue with Acts and the books that follow. Then go back and reread the complete New Testament.

2. "When and where should I read the Bible?" Whenever you need to! Wherever you are!

Get a small, readable copy of the Bible—perhaps *The Living Bible* or *The New King James Version*—that you can carry with you. That way, if you make an error in a project at work, you can take your Bible out of your desk and go on a five-minute break. If you feel you have been insulted while at a luncheon, you can pull your Bible out of the glove compartment of your car as you leave and spend some time reading God's words. If you are headed for an important meeting and are a little nervous, you can pause for a few minutes before you enter the room and read a passage of Scripture. Ask God to guide your reading.

Reading the Bible will get your mind off your present troubles and onto God's eternal truths. It will help you see your daily needs and hurts in clearer perspective. The Bible will truly provide peace for your soul.

3. *"What if I have difficulty concentrating?"* Read the Bible out loud. We human beings are egocentric enough to love the sound of our own voices. We listen to ourselves. When you read aloud, you are calling more of your senses into play. Your mind not only sees, it *hears* the Word of God.

Don't get bogged down in details. You can concentrate so hard on each word that you miss the message of the entire story or passage. Read the Bible as you would read a newspaper—as if it's a story someone is telling you. Take the whole. Read five verses and pause. Try to grasp an overall meaning for those five verses. If you don't understand anything you've read, read those same five verses again. Read and reread if you need to.

4. *"How can I keep the Bible passage I read alive in my spirit all day? How can I truly make the passage applicable to my life?"* As you read, watch for one verse that particularly stands out to you. Write it down on a card or scrap of paper and carry it with you all day. Put it in your purse or pocket. Place it on the dashboard of your car, by the sink, or on your desk. Read it over and over. Think about *why* this verse stood out to you. What made it "click" for your circumstances that particular day? Be aware that you are carrying the verse with you. Pause to look at it as you pass by your sink, hang up the

phone at your desk, or stop at a traffic light. You'll find the Word of God woven into the very fabric of your life.

In summary, I challenge you to make a commitment to read God's Word and to apply the Bible in practical, everyday ways to your life. I do not promise you that this will be an easy task. It is hard work.

The hardest work I know is to get into and stay in the habit of reading the Bible. It takes discipline, and we aren't disciplined people. You have to decide that reading the Bible matters above all else—that you will commit your mind to the task even if you miss a meal, don't get a school assignment finished, or don't get to bed on time. Our minds are ours to discipline, but we rarely do it.

A life in Christ isn't easy. Developing a habit of reading the Bible isn't easy, but it *can* be done and it's a challenge worth the effort. Exchanging discipline for a life transformed into the image of Christ—that's a bargain!

To find answers to life's questions, solutions to life's problems, and joy and peace for life's storms and pains . . . will *you* give five minutes a day for peace of mind?

WORD STUDIES

We have a friend who has been a great church worker for many years. She is really a marvelous woman, president of many women's groups, and active in a number of worthy projects. For many years she thought she couldn't study the Bible herself. She left interpretation of the Bible to her minister.

She said she was afraid to read the Bible, felt she didn't have enough time, thought hers was a ministry of helps and not Bible reading. She had many reasons for not studying the Bible, but the basic one was this: she didn't know that she *could* read and understand the Bible herself.

We talked with her about reading the Bible for just five minutes a day. She felt she just might understand five minutes worth, so she began to read daily. Soon she began planning a trip to Israel. Her husband was delighted. For years he had encouraged his wife to travel, but she never would agree. Now she wanted to get to know the author of the Bible better, and she wanted to know more about his homeland. The more she read her Bible, the more she realized that she didn't know Jesus in a personal way. She had heard about him for many years, but she didn't have

*Scripture references in this chapter are taken from the *King James Version.*

a personal relationship with him. Her husband began to have this desire for a deeper personal relationship with Jesus, too, and their life together began to revolve around Jesus and Bible study.

She told me once that Bible reading had become like potato chips for her—she couldn't take just one reading! She had a growing hunger for the Word, and over an eighteen-month period she began to read longer and longer passages, four and five times a day. She devoured the Word of God.

Equally important, she continually sought ways to apply the Bible to her life. She would say, "Now I understand this; let's see how I can put it to work in my life." You may have a Bible in your home and read it occasionally, but unless you *use it and put it into practice*, it has no real bearing on your life.

This pattern led our friend to desire to *study* the Bible. She suddenly had a great longing to know *everything* about the Bible—where all the books were located, what they said, how different concepts bridged the books of the Bible, the history of the Bible . . . *everything!* She was ready to do more than read and apply the Word. She wanted to study it in a more concentrated, deeper, and intense way.

She was ready to launch out into word studies!

What are the advantages of a word study? First, it's your own *personal* Bible study—made to order just for you and your interests and needs. Second, it's your introduction to the *entire Bible*. Word studies will get you playing the entire keyboard of the Word of God. Third, word studies are *concrete* and practical. They are methodical and organized.

Here's how you begin . . . .

Suppose you sit down for a brief rest from your daily routine. You have a cup of coffee and your Bible before you. You're ready for a five-minute reading. Your attention focuses on the cup in your hand. You ask, "I wonder what the Bible has to say about cups?" You launch into a word study about cups—and are surprised to find that the Bible has a lot to say about them. There's the cup of sorrow, the cup of grief, the cup of joy, and many other references.

Or you may be feeling sad or discouraged or punished. Use this feeling to get into a word study on "punishment."

You may find yourself launched into a word study as a result of your five-minute-a-day reading. A particular word may leap out at you from the page you read. You may stumble across words or concepts in your reading that will set you thinking about other incidents in the Bible that might be related. For example, as you're reading in the fifth chapter of Matthew (the Sermon on the Mount), you come across the phrase, "love your enemies." You may say, "What? I'm a new believer and God expects me to love my enemies? I'm not capable of doing that." Ask yourself, "What more does the Bible have to say . . ." Get ready to study the word "enemies." See what the Bible has to say about enemies and how to deal with them.

The key to word studies is the question that begins, "I wonder what the Bible has to say about . . ." The final word is your choice! That's why we say that a word study is the most personal Bible study you can have. The word you choose is from *your* experience, need, and curiosity.

How do you find out what the Bible has to say? It's at this point that you need to invest in a concordance. A concordance lists key words in the Bible in alphabetical order. Under each word you'll find key places in the Bible where that word is used. The references are listed in sequential order as they are found in the Bible—in other words, from the first book of the Old Testament to the last book of the New Testament.

spakest
art thou the man that *s.*? *Judg* 13:11
the silver thou *s.* of also. 17:2
words which thou *s.* *1 Sam* 28:21
thou *s.* also with thy mouth, and hast.
1 Ki 8:24; *2 Chr* 6:15
be verified which thou *s.* *1 Ki* 8:26
separate them, as thou *s.* by. 53
s. with them from heaven. *Neh* 9:13
then thou *s.* in vision to. *Ps* 89:19
since thou *s.* of him. *Jer* 48:27

span
a *s.* shall be the length, and a *s.* the.
Ex 28:16; 39:9

sparrow
s. hath found an house. *Ps* 84:3
I am as a *s.* alone upon the. 102:7

sparrows
are not two *s.* sold for ? *Mat* 10:29
are of more value than many *s.* 31
Luke 12:7
are not five *s.* sold for ? *Luke* 12:6

spat
spoken, he *s.* on ground. *John* 9:6

speak
(*Revisions frequently*, say *or* talk)
on me to *s.* to God. *Gen* 18:27, 31

EXAMPLE OF CONCORDANCE LISTING IN
CRUDEN'S COMPLETE CONCORDANCE

The back of your Bible may have an abbreviated concordance to help you get started. Separate concordances are well worth the purchase price, and are a wise investment. Or perhaps you could ask for a concordance as a gift. *Cruden's Complete Concordance* is a good, basic concordance for beginners. It's a handy size, not too detailed, and you can easily carry it with your Bible. *Young's* and *Strong's* are also good complete concordances. I suggest you invest first in a small concordance to get familiar with using one, and then progress to larger, more complete ones.

For many words, the list of Scripture references is long. Some span from Genesis to Revelation. You may want to look up only a few of the verses at one particular study time. A concordance gives a short quote from each Scripture to give you the basic context of the passage. You'll gain understanding by just reading down the list of one-line references, but I encourage you to look up as many Scriptures as you can. This will give you a more complete understanding of what the Bible has to say. This truly will get you into the *entire* Bible. You'll learn where all the books are located, what the abbreviations mean, and how the Bible is organized.

Most beginning piano students start with two notes, then one hand, then a few simple chords. Most of them can hardly wait until they are playing up and down the entire keyboard. The same is true for word studies. Even if you start with just a few verses, you'll find yourself wanting to play the entire keyboard of verses listed for a word.

As you look up the words, read a few Scriptures preceding and following the one listed in the concordance. This will help you keep the verse in context. You'll understand the entire passage better and have a more accurate interpretation of what the Bible is saying.

And now, let's get concrete and practical. You'll need paper and pencil for word studies. Word studies are 1, 2, 3, 4—itemized studies.

Paper and pencil, concordance, Bible in hand . . . and a word that interests you . . . you're ready to begin.

I'd like to share a word study with you to help launch you. I've chosen a word that is applicable to all of us: *money*.

MONEY

Are you aware of what money really is? It's a trade commodity. I need an item that you have; you need something that I have. I *trade* you what I have for what you need. In return I get what you have that I need. The exchange depends on mutual need.

In biblical times, gold and silver were the main trade items. Rings, bracelets, and other gold and silver objects were used as a medium of exchange in many countries. Other items have been used down through the years and in various cultures. Every culture has some type of money system.

The Bible has a great deal to say about money. Let's look at eight Scriptures in this study.

The first reference is Genesis *23:8-16*. It's important to read the verses in context, so let's take a look at the entire passage. Abraham's wife, Sarah, had died at the age of 127. Abraham is seeking a place to bury her body. Beginning in Genesis 23:8 . . .

And he communed with them, saying, If it be your mind that I should bury my dead out of my sight, hear me, and entreat for me to Ephron the son of Zohar, that he may give me the cave of Machpelah, which he hath, which is in the end of his field; for as much money as it is worth he shall give it me for a possession of a buryingplace amongst you. And Ephron dwelt among the children of Heth: and Ephron the Hittite answered Abraham in the audience of the children of Heth, even of all that went in at the gate of his city, saying, Nay, my lord, hear me: the field give I thee, and the cave that is therein, I give it thee; in the presence of the sons of my people give I it thee: bury thy dead.

And Abraham bowed down himself before the people of the land. And he spake unto Ephron in the audience of the people of the land, saying, But if thou wilt give it, I pray thee, hear me: I will give thee money *for the field; take it of me, and I will bury my dead there. And Ephron answered Abraham, saying unto him, My lord, hearken unto me: the land is worth four hundred shekels of silver; what is that betwixt me and thee? bury therefore thy dead.*

And Abraham hearkened unto Ephron; and Abraham weighed to Ephron the silver, which he had named in the audience of the sons of Heth, four hundred shekels of silver, current money *with the merchant.*

The land and cave became Abraham's permanent possession, and Abraham buried Sarah there.

Let's note several things about this passage. First, Abraham is dealing with strangers and he wants to be honest with them. He states his desire very plainly and tells *why* he wants to buy the field. The owners might have been happy for him to pay for the field, but perhaps they wouldn't have wanted it turned into a cemetery. Abraham was totally honest about his intent.

Second, he made certain that the business dealings were in the presence of the citizens of the town. He made his dealings public—no secret schemes in dark corners. Genesis 23:17, 18 tells us that the deal included the trees in the field. Abraham wanted it known publicly that the fruit of those trees and the area around the burial cave were his property.

And third, Abraham paid Ephron the exact amount suggested. He didn't quibble or bargain—or create any ill will in the process of the transaction. He paid the price asked of him. Now Ephron and the people of the town admired Abraham a great deal, and they wanted to *give* the field to him. It's important that Abraham didn't take advantage of their admiration. He didn't allow them to pay homage to him. He dealt squarely and fairly with them as if he were not famous or honored.

Finally, note that the real-estate transaction was a good deal for both Ephron and Abraham. Both parties were satisfied. The deal was totally fair. No one party was out to deceive or "rip off" the other. This is a major principle in God's economy: both parties in a transaction win!

This one passage of Scripture tells us quite a lot about money, doesn't it?

Our second reference is *Genesis 42:25*. This passage tells us how to deal with money within our families. It's important, again, to read this passage in context. Joseph was sold into slavery by his brothers. He rose through the ranks of slavery to become a leader in Pharaoh's house. Meanwhile, his homeland was hit with drought and famine. His family was starving, and the sons were sent to buy grain from Pharaoh's storehouse. The sons actually had to ask their brother, whom they had sold into slavery, for food to live—but they didn't recognize Joseph at the time. Joseph, however, recognized them. He ordered that their sacks be filled with grain. And then the Bible says:

Then Joseph commanded to fill their sacks with corn, and to restore every man's money *into his sack, and to give them provision for the way: and thus did he unto them.*

What a beautiful, loving way we have laid out before us here for dealing with our families in financial matters.

Joseph loved his family. He had forgiven his brothers, and he wanted them to survive the famine. He would have preferred to give the food to them, but he knew that for *their* benefit they should pay for the grain. That way they would not always feel dependent on him or indebted to him. The transaction between them was "pure business." But because Joseph loved his brothers, he found a *secret* way of returning their money to them.

Do you see what God is saying to us about dealing with family members? If you have relatives who want to buy something from you and you are willing for them to have it, you should *sell* it to them, even if you'd rather give it to them. This frees them from dependence on you. If you want to buy other gifts for them with the money, or return the money to them in a secret way—that's fine! And what a blessing to you if you do this! God's way keeps us from conniving and scheming for money and things, and it keeps us from using possessions and material goods as bait to win admiration or to control others.

In *Exodus 21:11* we see another principle at work:

And if he do not these three unto her, then shall she go out free without money.

We see again how important it is to read a Scripture in context. This passage is a part of the civil laws God gave to the Israelites. God said that when a woman was purchased as a slave, and the owner decided he didn't want her any longer, she was to go free, not to be sold again. Meanwhile he had fed her, clothed her, and given her a place to live. He had not taken away her honor or disgraced her. Yet she owed him nothing, and he owed her nothing.

Many times we are in a position to do something for others. We take care of their material needs—buy them clothes, help them find a decent place to live, or give them a meal. We help them get on their feet. The Bible says that when this period in a relationship draws to a close, nobody owes anybody anything. A line is drawn and both parties are free agents. The giver doesn't need to feel he owes the receiver any more money or possessions, and the receiver doesn't have to pay for the good things given to him. This really frees us from feeling obligated to others or from looking to others as a source of supply.

A fourth reference is *Deuteronomy 23:19, 20:*

Thou shall not lend upon usury [interest] to thy brother; usury of money, *usury of victuals, usury of any thing that is lent upon usury: Unto a stranger thou mayest lend upon usury; but unto thy brother thou shalt not lend upon usury: that the Lord thy God may bless thee in all that thou settest thine hand to in the land whither thou goest to possess it.*

Pretty straightforward, isn't it? God is giving laws to the Hebrew children in this passage. They are on their way to the promised land. God tells them they may not charge interest on loans made to their brothers. To us today, brothers would refer to members of our immediate family or to fellow-Christians. We may charge interest only on loans made to foreigners—those outside the family of God. The basic concept here is this: all money held by the children of God is really *God's property*. To charge interest to a fellow-believer is like charging yourself interest because you are both in the same body, with the same Lord as your head.

Five. Let's get over into the New Testament now. *Matthew 17:24-27* says:

And when they were come to Capernaum, they that received tribute money *came to Peter, and said, Doth not your master pay tribute? He saith, Yes. And when he was come into the house, Jesus prevented him, saying, What thinkest thou, Simon? of whom do the kings of the earth take custom or tribute? of their own children, or of strangers? Peter saith unto him, Of strangers.*

Jesus saith unto him, Then are the children free. Notwithstanding, lest we should offend them, go thou to the sea, and cast an hook, and take up the fish that first cometh up; and when thou hast opened his mouth, thou shalt find a piece of money: *that take, and give unto them for me and thee.*

This passage shows us that God is all-sufficient for us. Peter and Jesus were not really supposed to pay taxes. Capernaum was Peter's hometown, and he had every right to use the Temple to give God's message. Jesus let Peter know that he was not obligated to pay the taxes, but he also made a way to pay them so that nothing might stand in the way of Peter's work in the Temple.

Someone may require taxes, or payment, from you when you don't feel you owe him. God says to you, "I will supply the payment so that you will not offend anyone or stand in the way of my working through your life." God has great plans for us, and nothing is more important than seeing God's plans worked out in our lives. If getting into a fight over a payment—or going to court, making a scene, showing your temper, or carrying a placard—is going to keep you from getting on with God's work, it isn't worth it. Neither is spending excessive energy and creativity devising elaborate schemes to keep from paying taxes or utility bills. This wasted energy could be put to better use! God will provide a way for you to make the payments and get on with the task he's given you.

Our sixth reference is *Luke 19:12-15:*

A certain nobleman went into a far country to receive for himself a kingdom, and to return. And he called his ten servants, and delivered them ten pounds, and said unto them, Occupy till I come.

But his citizens hated him, and sent a message after him, saying, We will not have this man to reign over us.

And it came to pass, that when he was returned, having received the kingdom, then he commanded these servants to be called unto him, to whom he had given the money, that he might know how much every man had gained by trading.

This begins a story that continues through the next twelve verses. When the king returned to his province, he called the assistants for a report. The first man had invested the money, and he gave back ten times the original amount to the king. The king gave him ten cities to govern in the province. The next man also reported a gain. He had made five times the original amount. The king made him governor of five cities. But the third man brought back only the original sum. He said, "I was afraid, for you are a hard man to deal with." The king took his money away and gave it to the man who had earned the most.

Now this is a parable about our lives. It tells us that God isn't upset when Christians make money. It's a blessing to him! He wants us to prosper. He gives to us and wants us to multiply his gifts. If God gives you one portion and you can trade it and honestly turn it into ten portions . . . great! The point is to do the best you can and to invest for God.

We are also shown in this passage that we are to use the profits of our investments for God's glory. If God has given you a beautiful home, don't just enjoy it by yourself. Thank the Lord for it and use it to bless others—to provide a place for the wandering servant of God, to hold Bible studies and prayer meetings, to have dinners for friends who don't know the Lord so you can introduce them to Jesus. If God gives you a car, use it to pick up people and take them to church, or to run errands for your minister and his wife, or to take youth groups on special outings. These are the ways we *multiply* the gifts God has given us. This is an honor to God.

This passage also shows us that God recognizes our investments and generosity. The king gave his worthy servants the rulership of cities. In the same way, God will entrust to us certain responsibilities in his spiritual kingdom. He knows that if we are faithful in material things, we will be faithful to him in spiritual matters.

Finally, this passage tells us how to relate to our prosperous Christian brothers and sisters. Each assistant was given the same amount, but the one who worked the hardest and achieved the most was given the extra portion as both a reward and a responsibility. He had a responsibility to make God's money grow *again.* We should be happy for our prosperous neighbors. We should also pray for them. They are using their abilities for God's advantage, and God is giving them more *responsibility* as he gives them more riches.

Our seventh text is *Acts 8:18-22:*

And when Simon saw that through laying on of the apostles' hands the Holy Ghost was given, he offered them money, *saying, Give me also this power, that on whomso-*

ever I lay hands, he may receive the Holy Ghost. But Peter said unto him, Thy money *perish with thee, because thou hast thought that the gift of God may be purchased with* money. *Thou hast neither part nor lot in this matter: for thy heart is not right in the sight of God. Repent therefore of this thy wickedness, and pray God, if perhaps the thought of thine heart may be forgiven thee.*

Simon thought he could buy the power of God. He wanted to buy the anointing that was on the lives of Peter and John. He was saying to them, "I want to buy your ministry." God is telling us in this passage that we cannot buy a ministry or a call of God for our lives. God is the one who chooses special servants. God doesn't want mere money. He longs for hearts totally given to him. You can't buy a special place in God's kingdom. You can't buy houses in heaven with earthly money! God looks at the heart of a man, not his bank account.

The final reference I want to share with you is *1 Timothy 6:10.*

For the love of money *is the root of all evil: which while some coveted after, they have erred from the faith, and pierced themselves through with many sorrows.*

I encourage you to read the entire sixth chapter of Timothy. In this chapter, Paul warns Timothy about how some ministers preach only to make money. He tells Timothy to stay away from them. He tells Timothy that we should be satisfied if we have enough food and clothing—that greed causes men to engage in evil activities that hurt themselves, make them evil-minded, and eventually send them to hell. He encourages Timothy to:

Charge them that are rich in this world, that they be not high-minded, nor trust in uncertain riches, but in the living God, who giveth us richly all things to enjoy; that they do good, that they be rich in good works, ready to distribute, willing to communicate; laying up in store for themselves a good foundation against the time to come, that they may lay hold on eternal life (6:17-19).

The Bible clearly states in this chapter that the *love* of money is the root of all evil. Money isn't evil. The *love* of money—the spirit of greed—is what leads men to do evil things. You only need to read today's newspaper to see that this is so. Wars are fought over money. Families are divided over it. Murders are committed and stores are robbed because of greed.

Greed isn't limited to any one income bracket. Some people with the least money love it the most! Greed is a mind-set. It causes us to worry and to spend all our time and energy striving to get more money. Greed causes men and women to look at every item or activity through a dollar sign: "How much does it cost?" Greed causes us to hang on to our possessions. Money becomes an obsession to the greedy person.

God has a better idea! Live by faith and don't worry about storing up money. Be generous with what you have, and store up a real treasure for yourself in heaven.

These are only eight of the many references in the Bible about money. I encourage you to look up others. But what have we learned from these eight passages? This is where the pencil and paper come in handy.

When you look up a word in your concordance, write down the Scripture references. Then as you look up each passage, write down the key message or messages of that passage to you—that day, in your personal life. Here is how I would do that for the eight verses we have just studied:

MONEY

1. Genesis 23:9—*God wants me to deal openly and honestly in my business transactions. I should have witnesses for my transactions with strangers. I should be honest about why I want to buy an item or piece of property. I should not take advantage of people just because they admire me or want my friendship. My*

transactions should be of equal benefit for both parties.

2. Genesis 42:25—*God wants us to be businesslike with our relatives. He also wants us to be generous with our relatives.*

3. Exodus 21:11—*God doesn't want me to give to others in order that they will serve me or become dependent on me.*

4. Deuteronomy 23:19, 20—*God tells me not to charge interest on loans I make to fellow-Christians or to members of my family.*

5. Matthew 17:24—*God promises to supply my needs so that I don't need to waste my time squabbling with people about money or wallowing in tax regulations. I have more important things to do for Christ's kingdom!*

6. Luke 19:12—*God is pleased when I invest my money wisely and make a profit. I should use that profit to help and bless others.*

7. Acts 8:18—*I cannot buy my way into heaven or buy blessings from God. He looks at my heart.*

8. First Timothy 6:10—*Greed is the basis for much evil in our world. I should be happy if my basic needs are met and share my excess money with others.*

Did you find other aspects of these Scriptures speaking to your life?

Are you beginning to get a picture of God's system of economics? I think you'll have to agree that the Bible deals with money in a very practical, down-to-earth way.

Ready to try another quick study?

Let's turn our attention now to another word that plays a big part in each of our lives: *time.*

TIME

Time is something we all deal with, manage, and eventually run out of. Let's see what the Bible has to say about time in five key verses.

The first mention of the word "time" in the Bible is in *Genesis 18:9-14:*

And they said unto him, Where is Sarah thy wife? And he said, Behold, in the tent. And he said, I will certainly return unto thee according to the time of life, and lo, Sarah thy wife shall have a son. And Sarah heard it in the tent door, which was behind him.

Now Abraham and Sarah were old and well stricken in age; and it ceased to be with Sarah after the manner of women. Therefore Sarah laughed within herself, saying, After I am waxed old shall I have pleasure, my lord being old also?

And the Lord said unto Abraham, Wherefore did Sarah laugh, saying, Shall I of a surety bear a child, which am old? Is any thing too hard for the Lord? At the time appointed I will return unto thee, according to the time of life, and Sarah shall have a son.

Let's pick out the important parts of this passage as they relate to time. First, God made a promise to Abraham. That promise seemed impossible as man looked at it. Abraham and Sarah were too old to have a child—in the eyes of the natural man. Yet God's appointed time for them to have a child was still ahead. Abraham and Sarah *did* have a son. God's promise *was* fulfilled in their lives. This passage clearly points out to us that God has control of time. His timing may not be our timing, but his timing is always perfect. He's never too late or too early.

Furthermore, we see that God is not finished with us as long as we are alive. Many people feel that after their children are grown and gone from home, their purpose in life is past. Abraham and Sarah were well up in years, and yet God was just beginning a wonderful work in their lives. What marvelous lessons in this passage!

The next reference is *Exodus 9:13, 14*. This passage is in the midst of a discussion about the plagues that God brought on Egypt in order that Pharaoh would release the Hebrew children from bondage.

And the Lord said unto Moses, Rise up early in the morning, and stand before Pharaoh, and say unto him,

Thus saith the Lord God of the Hebrews, Let my people go, that they may serve me. For I will at this time send all my plagues upon thine heart, and upon thy servants, and upon thy people; that thou mayest know that there is none like me in all the earth.

Now read *Exodus 9:18:*

Behold, to morrow about this time I will cause it to rain a very grievous hail, such as hath not been in Egypt since the foundation thereof even until now.

These verses show us that God is very precise about time. He gives Moses an appointed, definite time to take Pharaoh the message. He tells when the hailstorm will begin. God knows his timetable and he deals in specifics. He knows what he has planned, and he executes his plans on time. This is a message to us to discipline our time. We should be ready to act at an appointed time and to be specific in our management of time.

A little later in *Exodus—21:18, 19*—we see that God values time. This passage deals with specific laws and commandments about how the Hebrew children were to live.

And if men strive together, and one smite another with a stone, or with his fist, and he die not, but keepeth his bed: If he rise again, and walk abroad upon his staff, then shall he that smote him be quit: only he shall pay for the loss of his time, and shall cause him to be thoroughly healed.

Loss of time is important to God. Time is valuable. The truth here is the basis for many insurance policies. It's also a key truth for each one of us: if our time is so valuable, it is worth taking a new look at how we spend it!

Our fourth passage on time is in *Luke 21:5-36.* This entire chapter deals with time. Here, time does not refer to the hour of the day or a time of life. It refers to God's eternal calendar. God has a plan and a timetable for all eternity. We live by that calendar as Christians on earth, and we will continue to live by that calendar after we die. Luke 21:5 sets the stage for the discussion between Jesus and his disciples:

And as some spake of the temple, how it was adorned with goodly stones and gifts, he said, As for those things which ye behold, the days will come, in the which there shall not be left one stone upon another, that shall not be thrown down. And they asked him, saying, Master, but when shall these things be? and what sign will there be when these things shall come to pass?

And he said, Take heed that ye be not deceived: for many shall come in my name, saying, I am Christ; and the time draweth near: go ye not therefore after them.

Jesus then explains the warnings that will precede that time and tells how the children of Israel should respond to the desolation. Jesus' words here were a prophecy. He is talking about the dispersion of Jewish people into all nations. This scattering happened in A.D. 70 under Titus, the Roman emperor. And in Luke 21:24 Jesus says:

And they shall fall by the edge of the sword, and shall be led away captive into all nations: and Jerusalem shall be trodden down by the Gentiles, until the times of the Gentiles be fulfilled.

Jesus was also looking ahead to the time when the nation of Israel would be reestablished and Jerusalem would be restored to the Jewish people. This has also happened—in our lifetime. The period of "Gentile triumph" of Israeli territory ended in 1947; and at the end of the Six-Day War in 1967, Jerusalem was regained by the Jewish people.

In Luke 21:25-30, Jesus tells what we can *now* expect. In verses 31 and 32 he says:

When they now shoot forth, ye see and know of your own selves that summer is now nigh at hand. So likewise ye, when ye see these things come to pass, know ye that the kingdom of God is nigh at hand.

The passage continues through verse 36. I encourage you to read the entire account. This chapter is as timely as your daily newspaper. It describes our world situation today! We are living in the time Jesus describes. It is a unique time on God's calendar. Just as Eve did not have anyone to whom she could turn to ask questions about having a baby, we don't have anyone to whom we can turn for specific direction and timetables. No one before us has lived in the final generation. Time as we know it is drawing to a close. We have nothing to fear in that. Jesus says his words remain true forever.

The Bible says only two things on earth last forever: God's Word and those who believe in Jesus. Since these are the only *eternal* things on earth, studying the Bible is the best thing we can be doing in the last days. Aren't you glad you're into God's Word!

We and Jesus are joint heirs of eternal life. His advice to us is in the first part of Luke 21:36:

Watch ye therefore, and pray always . . . .

We are to be in constant awareness that God is drawing time to a close. What an admonition to use our time wisely and to make every minute count for Christ.

This time I'd like for you to take the list of passages and write down what each meant to *you:*

TIME

1. Genesis 18:9—

2. Exodus 9:14—

3. Exodus 21:18, 19—

4. Luke 21:5-36—

Another key passage about time is in the third chapter of Ecclesiastes—especially the first fourteen verses. I encourage you to read this passage now and to summarize its meaning in your life today.

Ecclesiastes 3:1-14—

And now, where do you go from here? What is it that interests *you?*

Do you wonder if the Bible has anything to say about the foods we eat? Why not look up *spices?*

Are you interested in music? Look up *trumpet, harp,* or other instrument.

Are you planning a ski trip? Look up *snow!*

Is it spring? How about *flowers, seasons of the year,* or *colors?* How about *love?*

The choice is unlimited!

In closing this chapter on word studies, I'd like to share three brief thoughts with you. First, word studies help you know the personality of God. They tell you what God thinks about every aspect of life. The more word studies you do, the more you will know God and the closer you will be in your relationship with him. What a marvelous reason for studying the Bible!

Second, word studies will live with you all your life. You'll never outgrow them. You may do a word study on *love* this year, and find yourself doing a word study again on love in a couple of years. It will mean even more to you then, because you will have grown more in your experience with life and in your knowledge of the Bible. You may want to look up only a few references for a word now, and then look up more references in a few weeks or months. Word studies are always fresh and alive because you bring to them your current experience. They are in the present tense of your life. They are always applicable to where you are emotionally, spiritually, mentally, and physically.

Third, word studies make great devotional lessons. If you're asked to lead a devotional time in your club or group, you can always use a word study.

A final suggestion: keep the sheets of itemized Bible truths that result from your word studies. They are a handy reference in looking for quick guidance on very practical matters!

What are *you* going to study first? What word will *you* use to finish the sentence, "I wonder what the Bible has to say about . . ."?

SUBJECT STUDIES

Do you ever find yourself at a loss to know the opinion of God? Perhaps your friends have asked you, "What does God think about alcohol? Or drugs? What does God see as the ideal marriage? What does God think about welfare, prison systems, and governments? Does God have a master plan for the way we should live, eat, sleep, work, engage in recreation?" Subject studies will provide the answers for you!

Subject studies yield God's absolute opinion on any topic you can imagine. They provide answers to all the questions that begin, "What does God think about . . . ?"

The Bible encourages each of us to have the mind of Christ (Colossians 3:1, 2). The great purpose of subject studies is to so acquaint us with the mind of Christ—the perspective of God himself—that we begin to think as Christ thinks!

Philippians 2:5 says, "Let this same attitude and purpose and [humble] mind be in you which was in Christ Jesus." Philippians 4:8 continues this theme:

For the rest, brethren, whatever is true, whatever is worthy of reverence and is honorable and seemly,

*Scripture references in this chapter are from *The Amplified Bible.*

whatever is just, whatever is pure, whatever is lovely and lovable, whatever is kind and winsome and gracious, if there is any virtue and excellence, if there is anything worthy of praise, think on and weigh and take account of these things—fix your minds on them.

How do we get into subject studies? The key word is *contemplation.*

In order to contemplate, we need to establish a special time, place, mood, and frame of mind.

We can read the Bible five times a day on a catch-and-snatch basis. As we move through our daily lives, we can steal five minutes here and five minutes there for spiritual feedings. When we do word studies, we can make them long or short. We can look up concordance references at different times. The word studies are straightforward, each reference yielding specific and readily identifiable truths.

Subject studies, however, demand a quiet atmosphere, an environment where you can relax without interruption. Contemplation requires a time for the mind and soul to "wander" under the guidance of the Holy Spirit.

This need not be a *long* period of time—perhaps only twenty or thirty minutes. Make an "appointment" with God each week—just as regularly as you schedule your appointment with your hairdresser or golf partner. You might set aside a time when the baby is napping or the casserole is in the oven, or use the time you are on an airplane, or find a time in the late evening or early morning in the quiet of your home.

The first practical step in getting launched into a subject study is to *make* the time and place. You might want to establish one specific chair or one corner of the garden as your "contemplation setting." This environment will become so familiar to you that it won't distract you; it will *help* you concentrate.

Seek a place of quiet and peace. Search out a time when you can read the Bible without interruption. Unplug the phone if you can. Determine within yourself that you will not allow yourself to think about anything other than the passage of the Bible in front of you. Have paper and pencil handy to record your ideas.

Begin to relax in your inner person, and don't feel guilty for taking this time apart from your daily chores. Ask the Holy Spirit to guide your thoughts.

Dear Jesus,
I want to know more about you. I have to know your opinions so I can live by them. Please help me remove from my mind the cares of this day and help me to concentrate on your Word and your thoughts. Cause your Holy Spirit to lead me into the truth of this subject matter today. I will obey. In Jesus' name I pray. Amen.

And then begin to read, continuing on in the same place you have been in your five-minute reading schedule.

As you read a passage in the Bible, stop after three or four verses—at least a paragraph—and begin to contemplate. How do we contemplate? Here are some practical tips to help you reflect on the Scriptures:

1. Seek out key words within a passage. Identify the key ideas. Number them if you wish. Underline them, or write out the key sentences on a piece of paper. Here is an example from Matthew 4 (KJV).

of the devil.
2 And when he had fasted forty days and forty nights, he was afterward ahungered.
3 And when the tempter came to him, he said, If thou be the Son of God, command that these stones be made bread.
4 But he answered and said, It is written, Man shall not live by bread alone, but by every word that proceedeth out of the mouth of God.

word, not bread, most important

2. Look up individual words and names of places that may be unfamiliar to you. Use both a dictionary and a Bible dictionary, which is a very useful tool to have in subject studies. I recommend the Davis, Halley's or Douglas Bible dictionaries or handbooks.

3. Look up the key words and related words in a concordance.

4. Identify synonyms and other words that are related to the key words you have identified in the passage. In the last chapter, we focused on the word money *for a word study. A host of related ideas surround the concept of money: leasing, borrowing, giving, stealing, lending, investing. These words all relate to the* function *of money. There are also a group of nouns that are related (wealth, riches, poverty, possessions, greed) and a group of adjectives that describe people and money (generous, stingy, poor, rich, greedy).*

5. Identify what the passage is not *saying. Take the "opposites approach." What are the opposites of the key words you have identified in the passage?*

6. Identify the ingredients necessary to make the objects *described in a passage. For example, identify what is required to make bread, a cross, pearls, or gold. This also applies to the ingredients for certain attitudes or conditions. What causes us to be jealous or joyous?*

7. Ask yourself, "How does this relate to me? What in my life's experience is most like the incident or the key point of the passage?" Can you identify with the feeling of the passage? Have you ever been in a situation similar to the one described? Have you ever felt the way the Bible writer seems to feel?

8. Summarize your contemplation to this point. What is the passage's main topic or subject? What is the Bible saying to you?

9. Make notes about what you already know—have heard, read, or believe—about the general topic. Ask the Holy Spirit to bring related verses to your remembrance. Jot down other Scriptures you have come across in your five-minute readings. Jot down teachings you have heard in the past on the subject. Recall incidents that might be examples of the Bible's truth in the passage. These may be incidents or circumstances in your past, or happenings in the lives of friends.

10. When you have thought through this passage thoroughly, begin to compare past teachings, ideas, and incidents to other references in the Bible. Begin to evaluate the opinions of others in light of the Word of God. Do their ideas agree with what the Bible has to say? Have you understood correctly?

You may need several days—even a week—of twenty- or thirty-minute sessions in order to make it through all ten steps of contemplation described here. You may not go through the process in numerical order as it is listed above, but by the end of your contemplation you will probably have touched on all ten approaches.

At the conclusion of the process, you will understand a passage of Scripture as you have never before understood it.

You will have discovered God's unchanging opinion on a certain topic.

You will begin to gain a sense of independence *for yourself in the Bible. You will no longer need to rely solely on others to interpret the Bible or the mind of Christ for you. You will begin to have an understanding of the Word of God for yourself—you will be able to evaluate the ideas of others in light of God's eternal and divine principles.*

You will begin to see topics as more than itemized lists of ideas. Subjects will become more like circles: well-rounded areas of thought. These circles will be seen in technicolor, filled with detail, and made alive with feeling! You will receive deeper and deeper insights into the mind of Christ as you engage in subject studies.

Contemplation puts us into a position to receive communication from God. It creates an atmosphere and a situation in which God can speak to us in the still, quiet areas of our hearts.

Let's do a subject study. Let us assume for a moment that you have been reading in Matthew. You have been doing word studies on key words that stand out to you in your daily reading and in your everyday experiences. You have set aside a portion of today for *contemplation* on a passage of the Bible. You have come to Matthew 18 and you read in the first four verses:

At that time the disciples came up and asked Jesus, Who then is [really] the greatest in the kingdom of heaven? And He called a little child to Him and put him in the midst of them, and said, Truly, I say to you, unless you repent (change, turn about) and become like little children [trusting, lowly, loving, forgiving] you can never enter the kingdom of heaven at all. Whoever will humble himself therefore, and becomes [trusting, lowly, loving, forgiving] as this little child, is the greatest in the kingdom of heaven . . . .

Here is how *my* contemplation process would flow for this passage . . . .

These are the key words and ideas that stand out to me in this passage as I read it today:

loving child
we become little children through repentance
the only way to enter the kingdom of heaven is to become as a little child
those who are like little children become the greatest in the kingdom of heaven

I ask myself, "What does it mean to be a child? What are the attributes of children?" We were all children once. God knows this is something we should be able to understand easily. The passage says that children are trusting. God is saying to me that we must put our total trust—and sense of completeness and security—in him.

I recall sociology studies that I have read. One of these studies reports that even in times of war or great natural disaster, children come through traumatic situations emotionally unscarred if they have at least one parent or adult with whom they feel secure. Children do not "fall apart" in catastrophe if they are in the presence of an adult who loves them and is at peace with himself. The child has a source of reference that transcends the trauma. Sociology studies also tell us that children can survive with very little food and still remain healthy *if* they live without fear and experience the holding, caring love of an adult.

I know this to be true in my own life. When I was a child, my hometown was flooded. Eventually, only the rooftops were above water. The flood caused great damage to the lower floor of our three-story home and brought great distress to our neighbors. Yet the only memories I have of that flood are happy memories. I recall times of paddling around the area with my father in our little rowboat. We would check out the flood level in different areas, find people to assist, and make ourselves useful to the authorities. I felt as safe as could be because my father was in the boat with me, and he had a confident, cheery attitude. It's only now, when I look back on that incident as an adult, that I realize what a tragedy the flood must have been for my family and neighbors.

These ideas trigger another question: "How can *I*, as a parent, provide a sense of security and trust in God for my children?" In looking up *child* in the concordance, I find a reference in Deuteronomy 6:5-9:

And you shall love the Lord your God with all your [mind and] heart, and with your entire being, and with all your might. And these words, which I am commanding you this day, shall be [first] in your own mind and heart; [then] you shall whet and sharpen them, so as to make them penetrate, and teach and impress them diligently upon the [minds and] hearts of your children, and shall talk of them when you sit in your house, and when you walk by the way, and when you lie down, and when you rise up . . . .

This passage tells me that I am to tell my children about God from the moment they are born. I am to talk with them about Jesus and pray with them. I must *not* hide my love for the Lord from my children.

The earlier the seeds of faith are planted in a child's spiritual life through Bible stories, the greater the opportunity for the seeds to grow. The Holy Spirit will bring to remembrance the truths learned at the earliest memories. These ideas actually become the foundation on which the child's psyche develops. Eventually, the child will feel he or she is starving unless he has a diet of spiritually nourishing food.

I recall from my travels in other countries how different nationalities have different foods. An oriental child raised on a diet primarily of rice will find that same rice diet satisfying to his body when he reaches adulthood. The child raised on meat and vegetables, however, would find a rice-based diet inadequate as an adult. This same principle holds true for our inner growth.

A key word to me in the Deuteronomy passage is *diligently.* When I look up diligent in a dictionary I come across such words as painstaking, active, busy, and "perseveringly attentive." The opposites listed are lazy, careless, indifferent.

As a parent, then, I am admonished by this Scripture to be constant and attentive in my parental role. A parent is never to let up or take a vacation from child-rearing. The parent's example and teaching must be continuous and consistent. I recall that my children's pediatrician once said to me, "The most consistent attribute of children is inconsistency." Children are forever growing and changing. The greatest gift we parents can give to our children is consistency. Maturity includes *consistency.*

And then the passage goes on to give me practical ways of teaching my children. I am to talk with my children about the Lord when we sit together and walk together, and when we lie down and rise up. I am to live out my Christian commitment so my children can see *daily* that Christ is important in my life and that he is the foremost reason for my being. I am to make our home a lovely place of peace and faith—a witness to all the world that our home is inhabited by Jesus.

Just reading this passage in Deuteronomy impressed me anew that God does not want our children to fall into sin. His desire is for our children to grow up loving him every day of their lives.

Realizing this brings to my mind the story of Hannah and Samuel in the first three chapters of 1 Samuel. Hannah had been barren for many years, and Samuel was the direct answer to prayer in her life. In 1 Samuel 1:26 we read:

> *Hannah said, Oh, my lord [Eli]! As your soul lives, my lord, I am the woman who stood by you here, praying to the Lord. For this child I prayed, and the Lord has granted my petition made to Him. Therefore I have given him to the Lord; as long as he lives he is given to the Lord.*

Hannah dedicated Samuel to the Lord with her whole heart. Samuel was even allowed to live in the Temple with Eli, the priest, when he was just a child. It was there that Samuel grew and was "in favor both with the Lord and with men." One night God called to Samuel in an audible voice. Samuel was given a very special mission on earth: to anoint Israel's first king.

This passage tells me how we are to dedicate our children to God and to release them for God's work. We are to raise our children to serve God—not so they might serve us when we are old. We are to be independent from our children when they reach maturity; we must prepare ourselves to let our children leave the nest.

When my friend Ann's children were small, many times she awoke them with a glass of orange juice and prayer. She prayed at mealtimes with her children, not only for the food but for the tests at school and the relationships they had with their teachers and classmates. She made a habit of strong prayer and words about the Lord as she drove them to school: "Honey, I know God is going to take care of you today. No matter what happens, I'm going to be here loving and supporting you. The Lord loves you. I pray that guardian angels will watch over you every minute of today and protect your mind from things that are displeasing to God."

She'd greet her children when they came home from school with a word about what the Lord had done for her or meant to her in a practical way during that day. Several nights a week she and her husband, Alan, would have a family time together. They'd gather in their son's room one night, let him pray first, and then all the rest of them would pray while he went to sleep. The next time they'd gather in their daughter's room. When the children were grown, the children would pray for Ann and Alan as they'd go to sleep! (What a secure feeling—to fall asleep listening to the prayers of your family!)

As they would deal with adults about accepting Jesus as their Savior, Ann and Alan made it the children's responsibility to pray for the children of that family. They also sang with their children. Even though the children couldn't carry a tune, Ann would encourage them to make up songs out of their favorite Scriptures.

Ann and Alan's children grew up knowing that Jesus is alive and that he cares about us every minute of every day. They had a great freedom in expressing themselves to the Lord. The children are now adults, and they have never rebelled against God or turned away from loving and serving him.

The passage in 1 Samuel also triggers a question in my mind: "How great is the influence of a parent over a child?" Words closely related to children are *parent, mother, father, son,* and *daughter.* These are "surrounding concepts" on the subject of children. In looking up these words in a concordance, I come across these Scriptures:

> *Forty-two years old was Ahaziah when he began his one year reign in Jerusalem. His mother was Athaliah granddaughter of Omri. He also walked in the ways of the house of Ahab, for his mother was his counselor to do wickedly. So he did evil in the sight of the Lord like the house of Ahab; for they were his counselors after his father's death, to his destruction* (2 Chronicles 22:2-4).

(Here is a forty-two-year-old man who is still listening to his mother, and unfortunately her advice was evil and led to his downfall!)

Jeremiah 9:13, 14 says:

. . . they have forsaken My law which I set before them, and have not listened and obeyed My voice or walked in accordance with it, but have walked stubbornly after their own heart and after the Baals, as their fathers *taught them . . . .*

(Fathers influence their children most by what they emphasize in their own lives. If fishing is your passion, it will likely be your son's also . . . or he'll *hate* it with a passion.)

I also recall Scripture passages that tell us that young children are supposed to do as their parents say. Exodus 20:12 is one of the Ten Commandments:

Regard (treat with honor, due obedience and courtesy) your father and mother, that your days may be long in the land the Lord your God gives you.

Ephesians 6:1-6 continues this theme:

Children, obey your parents in the Lord [as His representatives], for this is just and right. Honor (esteem and value as precious) your father and your mother; this is the first commandment with a promise: That all may be well with you and that you may live long on the earth. Fathers, do not irritate and provoke your children to anger—do not exasperate them to resentment—but rear them [tenderly] in the training and discipline and the counsel and admonition of the Lord.

I ask, "How do I discipline my child without provoking anger?" I recall the age-old saying, "Spare the rod and spoil the child." I question this saying and search for the proverb on which it is based: Proverbs 13:24.

He who spares his rod [of discipline] hates his son, but he who loves him diligently disciplines and punishes him early.

The words "loves him diligently" stand out to me. We are always to couch the discipline of our children with *love* . . . a diligent love. Love must always be the motivation for disciplining our children. We are not to strike our children in anger, or to strike them without a reason steeped in love. Such punishment only provokes our children to resentment.

I have a close friend who has grown children who are as close to the Lord as any parent could desire. This is how she and her husband approached the discipline of their children when the children were young. They determined to punish their children on three accounts:

1. If they were about to do something that would hurt themselves physically, psychologically, or spiritually;
2. If they did something to hurt others;
3. If they did something to hurt or destroy property.

When their children would do something they felt wasn't right, they would send them to their rooms. This gave the parents time to cool off and to ask themselves before God, "Is this something that is displeasing to God? Is this something that is dangerous for the future welfare of my child? Or is it just that I'm angry because my pride as a parent has been injured?"

When they honestly felt their children needed to learn a lesson for their own safety, the safety of others, or the safety of property, they could enter the situation calmly, feeling hurt also, and say, "I must punish you so that you won't forget this incident." When the children were older, the parents would often add, "What would *you* see as a punishment that would so impress this situation on your mind that you'll never forget it or want to do this again?"

As I contemplate further, I begin to look at the source of children: mothers and fathers. The subject of children includes the relationship of husbands and wives. My soul wanders to the opening chapters of the Bible, and the narrative about Adam and Eve in Genesis 2—4. Key truths stand out:

Adam was created from dust. He was formed and shaped by the hand of God. A man must remain pliable in God's hands. Eve was made from Adam's rib—to provide inner protection *for the heart of her husband while Adam provided the physical, external strength for their home.*

Eve is given her name by Adam. Her name means life-spring, and she is described in Genesis 3:20 as the "mother of all living." This description is given to Eve long before she conceived and bore Cain! God sees women then and now as wives and mothers . . . as helpmates and as those who create, nurture, protect, and provide love in our world. I recall incident after incident in my life in which unmarried women served (helped) others and were mothers to unloved orphans, prisoners, impoverished, widowed, uneducated, hungry, and unclothed. Women have a great capacity for serving others and for loving the lonely—be they rich or poor.

Adam's curse was to provide for his family. No matter what job a man has, he works under great strain and tension to meet the demands of being a father. So if the father is so busy at his job that he has very little time with his family, we must realize that this is the way the father shows his concern and love for his family and fulfills his curse.

Eve's curse was to bear her children in sorrow, to bear the burden of them all the days of her life, and to obey her husband.

The curse given to the serpent (Satan) was woman. It was from a woman—a virgin—that Jesus was born. His life, death, and resurrection have bruised the head of Satan forever. Women have been given a responsibility to keep the serpent out of the lives of their husbands and children. Some of the ways women can do this are by guiding the conversations, music, books, and media programs that take place in the home. They can do this without fuss or worry. A woman doesn't even need to break stride as she steps on and snaps off the head of the serpent in her home.

Many other truths stand out in these chapters in Genesis, but my contemplative mind wanders to the children of Adam and Eve: Cain and Abel. And from there to other brothers and sisters in the Bible: Moses, Aaron, and Miriam (Exodus 15:20 and Numbers 12); James and John, the sons of Zebedee, and their petition in Mark 10:35-38; Jacob and Esau (Genesis 25:19-34; 27); Isaac and Ishmael (Genesis 16, 17, 21, 22).

This brings me pretty much full circle in my contemplation today on the topic of children. I am back to the place where I am to become as a child and I am to look to God as my heavenly Father. That process involves *repentance*, and that is yet another key word in my original passage in Matthew 18.

Tomorrow, perhaps, I will begin my contemplation on the passage with the concept of repentance.

Do you see how the contemplative process works in our subject studies of the Bible? Do you see why it is important that you are reading the Bible regularly and doing word studies before you begin a subject study? You must have some familiarity with the Bible so you can recall related passages and incidents. You must be in the habit of seeing the Bible as relating to *your* life—where you are and who you are in Christ *today*.

Let's take another example, beginning this time with a passage a little earlier in Matthew. Matthew 11:28-30 says:

Come to Me, all you who labor and are heavy-laden and over-burdened, and I will cause you to rest—I will ease and relieve and refresh your souls. Take My yoke upon you, and learn of Me; for I am gentle (meek) and humble (lowly) in heart, and you will find rest—relief, ease and refreshment and recreation and blessed quiet—for your souls. For My yoke is wholesome (useful, good)—not harsh, hard, sharp or pressing, but comfortable, gracious and pleasant; and My burden is light and easy to be borne.

For this passage, I'd like to ask you leading questions that may guide your own contemplation:

What are the key words you see in this passage? What are the key ideas?

(Two of the key ideas to me are that Jesus' yoke is easy, and we are to come to Jesus when we are heavy-laden and overburdened.)

Have you ever been heavy-laden? (I have a friend who struggles with a problem of being overweight and when she reads this passage she feels she knows *exactly* what heavy-laden means!)

Have you ever felt overburdened and overworked—exhausted to the core?

Well, Jesus seems to say that he will ease and relieve and refresh us . . . and then he turns right around and says we are to take his yoke upon us!

What do you know about a yoke? Look it up in a dictionary, or better still, a Bible dictionary.

Did you know that a yoke is for *two* animals? Jesus said it was *his* yoke—he's willing to share the burden with us.

Do you realize that a yoke unites two animals for the purpose of *work?* Yokes exist to make tasks accomplishable. Jesus is going to be there in our *work*—even in the everyday, earn-a-living jobs. Our lives are filled with tasks—work to do as unto the Lord. He promises to be there with us.

Then Jesus says he is meek—gentle, humble, lowly in heart. What else have you read in the Bible about the nature of Jesus?

What does it mean to be meek?

Do you recall how Jesus healed the sick? Surely he was a compassionate man. Do you recall how Jesus drove the moneychangers out of the Temple and how he consistently outwitted the scribes and Pharisees? Surely he was a bold, wise, quick-witted man. Meek does *not* mean that Jesus was timid, dumb, or without charisma.

What does meek mean then? The dictionary says it means patient, long-suffering, kind. We see this in the healing and teaching ministry of Jesus.

Meek also means that Jesus was so secure in the

knowledge of who he was that he was free to serve. He was not defensive. He was not aggressive. He knew his purpose on earth and he went on his way, daily fulfilling that purpose.

This passage tells us to be like Jesus—secure in the knowledge of who we are. We are to be meek. When we know who we are, and when we know the task we are to do in life, then we find that our burdens are lighter, easier to bear. We become a "matched team" with Jesus, both of us doing the same work under the same yoke.

Stop to think about a yoke for a minute. Do you know what the ingredients are for a yoke?

Note, too, that Jesus was raised in a carpenter's home and he himself was a carpenter for many years. Jesus would know how to make a yoke. He was a craftsman. He would be able to make a yoke to fit the shoulders of an ox perfectly, and that is the way yokes are fashioned. Each yoke is individually crafted to fit the specific team of oxen that is going to use it so there is no chafing on the shoulders of the beasts. No two yokes are alike. Jesus knows how to design *our* yokes so that they are not harsh, hard, sharp, or pressing—but comfortable, gracious, and pleasant. Jesus would also know how to make a *cross*, wouldn't he? (See Luke 9:23.)

Have you identified the central theme of this passage? For me, today, during this time of contemplation, the theme is suffering. Can you identify other key words that are close to suffering? How about . . .

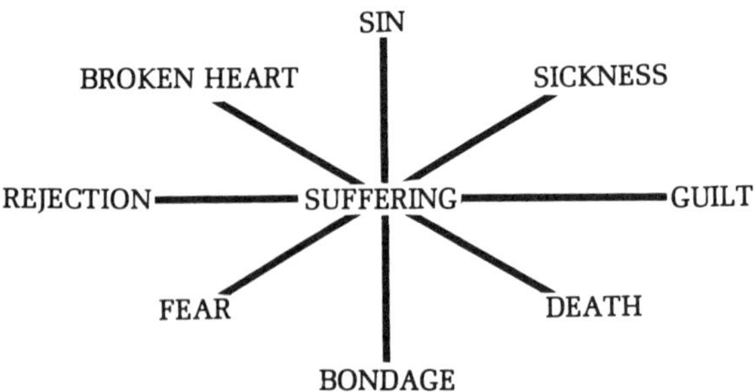

Can you identify the opposites of those states?

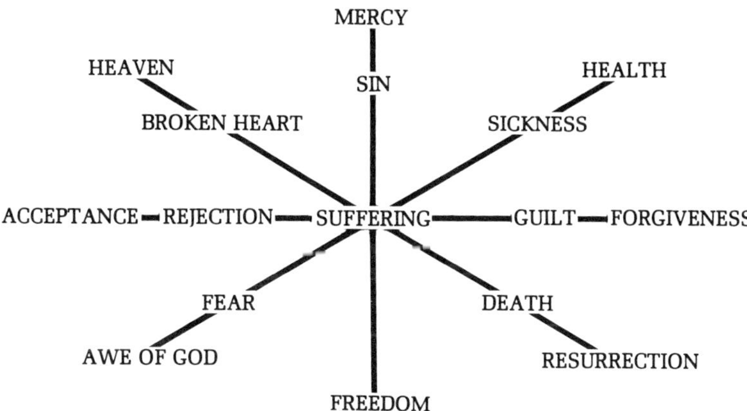

This graphic wheel represents conditions of suffering, *and* the conditions of redemption! A word study following one of the spokes of the wheel would reveal how we overcome various types of suffering in our lives, wouldn't it?

Are you familiar with Psalm 6, which describes the nature of suffering? The psalm speaks of both physical and spiritual suffering. Read that psalm to see what key concepts stand out to you. Can you identify with verse 6? "I am weary with my groaning; all night I soak my pillow with tears; I drench my couch with my weeping."

Think about the crucifixion of Jesus. Think about the Garden of Gethsemane and how Jesus bore our *psychological* suffering there. (See Luke 22:39-46.) Think about how Jesus was beaten and nailed to a cross to bear our *physical* suffering. His bleeding to death on the Cross for our sins was the sacrifice that makes our *spiritual* life and freedom possible.

You may also think about suffering you have experienced in childbirth. See Genesis 35:16; Isaiah 13:8, 42:14; and John 16:21.

You may think you have suffered greatly by being neglected or left alone. See Acts 6:1 or 9:39.

You may have suffered over the loss of a child. David certainly suffered over the loss of Absalom (2 Samuel 18:5—19:1).

You may have suffered over the wrongdoing of a child. Adam and Eve also suffered in this way with Cain

(Genesis 4). Perhaps you will recall the story of the prodigal son in Luke 15:11-32.

Think about teachings you have heard about suffering. Do you know why we suffer? Jesus' disciples asked about this when Jesus encountered a man who was blind from birth. The story is recorded in John 9. They asked, "Who sinned, this man or his parents, that he should be born blind?"

In John 9:3 Jesus replies, "It was not that this man or his parents sinned; but he was born blind in order that the workings of God should be manifested—displayed or illustrated—in him."

Jesus tells us that when an individual is sick or handicapped, it is not necessarily directly because of that person's sin. He suffers as part of our general human condition on earth. Sin, sickness, and death came into the world with Satan. Christ came to *overcome* these evils (Romans 8).

You may be asking, "How am I to cope with suffering?" In looking up suffering in the concordance, you'll find 1 Peter 2:20:

[After all] what kind of glory [is there in it] if when you do wrong and are punished for it you take it patiently? But if you bear patiently with suffering *[which results] when you do right and that is undeserved, it is acceptable and well-pleasing to God.*

And 2 Timothy 1:12, 13 says:

And this is why I am suffering *as I do. Still I am not ashamed, for I know—I perceive, have knowledge of and am acquainted with Him—Whom I have believed (adhered to and trusted in and relied on), and I am [positively] persuaded that He is able to guard and keep that which has been entrusted to me and which I have committed [to Him], until that day.* Hold fast and follow the pattern of wholesome and sound teaching which you have heard from me, in [all] the faith and love which are [for us] in Christ Jesus.

How about our role when *others* suffer? First Corinthians 12:26 tells us what we are to do for others who are suffering:

And if one member suffers, all the parts [share] the suffering; *if one member is honored, all the members [share in] the enjoyment of it.*

As Christians, we each are part of a whole. The Bible says we are to be so close that we are like one person (or body) (Romans 12:4, 5). What do we know about bodies that are in pain? Have you ever had a sore toe or a hangnail? When even the least part of our bodies is in misery, the entire body suffers! The same is true for the body of believers. We need each other, and we need to hang together through thick and thin.

In 1 Corinthians 13, we see that love has a part in suffering:

Love suffers long—and is kind in the midst of it.
Love does not envy or act pushy.
Love bears and endures all things—good and bad—without behaving in an unseemly manner.

And a few chapters earlier, in 1 Corinthians 10:13, we read:

For no temptation—no trial regarded as enticing to sin [no matter how it comes or where it leads]—has overtaken you and laid hold on you that is not common to man—that is, no temptation or trial has come to you that is beyond human resistance and that is not adjusted and adapted and belonging to human experience, and such as man can bear.

But God is faithful [to His Word and to His compassionate nature], and He [can be trusted] not to let you be tempted and tried and assayed beyond your ability and strength of resistance and power to endure, but with the temptation He will [always] also provide the way out—*the means of escape to a landing place—that you may be capable and strong and powerful patiently to bear up under it.*

These are comforting words, aren't they? We are not given temptations, trials, or suffering beyond "human resistance" and "such as man can bear." Jesus does not give us a yoke that is too heavy for us to carry. He doesn't put us into fields that are too difficult to plow. We are able to "bear up under it." We will feel needed, worthy, and have a sense of accomplishment as we finish plowing the fields set before us.

We are to follow the sound teaching of the Bible and *rest* in the faith and love which are in Jesus Christ our Lord!

And that brings us back to our yoke, doesn't it? We have a task to do. We know that Jesus has joined in this task with us, and that it is not beyond us. We know who we are—that we are to be of the same nature as Jesus, who has triumphed over the greatest suffering mankind has ever known. We take courage when we know who we are and what we have to do—and that Jesus is with us forever. His presence and his promises make the burden light.

Can you see how contemplative thought flows, how it moves from one area of our knowledge and experience to another?

Can you see the importance of having a quiet, uninterrupted, comfortable time in which these deep and reflective thoughts can unfold naturally as God speaks to us?

Many of my friends have remarked how subject studies were the turning point for them in their study of the Bible. It is at this level of study that we begin to truly understand the deeper meanings of the Bible and to see a constant reflection of our lives in the Word of God and of the Word of God in our lives.

As a very practical suggestion, extend your contemplation to times that seem boring to you: as you drive on the way to work or to shop, as you jog, garden, or shovel snow, or as you do routine chores around the house or take a bath. Make these routine activities come alive for you mentally by thinking about the Word of God.

Our friend Ken is a genius—a brilliant scientist whose mind amazes all who meet him. He was once a devout atheist.

Shortly after Ken's wife became a believer, he decided to investigate the Bible. This led to a dramatic conversion. He read the Bible from cover to cover in about a week, and within two weeks after that he had given his first Bible study presentation!

Ken was amazed that all the truth he had ever sought was available in one book. Even more, he was amazed that *anyone* could seek out the truth of the Bible for himself.

Ken launched out into several subject studies. First, he tackled the various doctrines of the Bible—such as atonement, resurrection, repentance. In this way he began to be able to distinguish between the eternal principles of God and the inventions of man. Next, Ken delved into the writings of theologians down through the ages. He read the original treatises of all the giants of theology over a period of a year. He compared their opinions with the direct Word of God.

Not all of us are like Ken, with a mind that can absorb so quickly and encompass so much in such a short period of time. But I believe we all must reach the conclusions that Ken reached after his exhaustive studies:

Only *the Word of God is* holy. *All other books—all ideas of men—are subject to the divinely inspired Bible.*

Because of that, the Bible needs no defense by man. It needs no elaboration or analogy. The Bible stands on its own authority.

Are you ready to engage in a subject study of your own? Perhaps you'd like to pursue the themes of "children" or "suffering" further. Many unexplored avenues of thought remain in both of these areas. In fact, you will find yourself coming back to certain subjects again and again throughout your life to discover new and deeper truths.

The more you know the Bible, the more correlations you will be able to make among Scriptures, the more experience you will have to add to your Scripture analysis, and the easier it will be for you to identify the key meaning of specific passages.

The Sermon on the Mount (chapters 5, 6, 7 of Matthew) will provide many launching points for you in subject studies.

Or perhaps a word study will expand and expand in your mind until it becomes a subject study. Or perhaps you will come across a passage of Scripture in your five-minute reading that will trigger a contemplative session.

However you launch into the deeper truths of the Bible, recognize that this is the point where you begin to be able to interpret the Bible for yourself and to have the "mind of Christ" within you. It is in subject studies that you will discover God's opinions and his perfect plan for your life *today!*

JOURNEY STUDIES

My husband once said, "We make only two kinds of decisions in life: big ones and little ones. The problem is that we don't know how to tell the difference as we are making the decision. We only know in retrospect. Sometimes *no* decision is a big decision."

How true! Certain decisions that we make in our daily life often set our course for years to come. Life flows on in a new direction. We live out our lives on a new path.

All of us are on a journey through life. We choose different roads. We see different scenery and experience different situations along the way. Statistics tell us that Americans move an average of once every three years. We are all "in process." Today will flow into tomorrow. Today's choices will affect tomorrow's choices and so on and so on and so on.

Often, along the way, we run into detours. Things don't turn out as we had thought or planned. We begin to ask:

Where did I foul up?
What do I do now?
What can I do to turn things around?
How can I add new excitement and meaning to my life?

*Scripture references in this chapter are from the *New American Standard Bible.*

What would Christ's attitude be toward this situation?
What is my destination five years from now if I stay on this road?

The Bible tells the story of many journeys—both journeys of individuals and the journey of the children of God. A study of these journeys can help us answer life's nagging questions. They help us see that life happens in stages. Journeys are taken in increments. We cover ground a step at a time: one foot up and one foot down.

Be sure not to miss the beauty along the way! Learn the roads to take so you don't end up on rocky ledges. Keep the roadmap—your Bible—handy.

Journey studies also help us see that *situations do change*. No circumstance or situation lasts forever. That goes for the bad times, but also the good times. Many people think that specific circumstances are all they need for happiness—enough money, social prestige, or power. They work hard to achieve their goals, and then when they arrive at their destination they find emptiness. They discover that no object or position on earth, no matter how great, lasts forever.

Journey studies help us gain a new perspective on life. They help us see that we are like other human beings—those we live with on the earth today and those who have lived before us. Journey studies also help us to learn from others about how to deal with problems we encounter along life's paths.

One of the most meaningful journey studies I know is the life of Joseph.

The journey of Joseph begins in Genesis 37 and lasts until the end of the book, chapter 50. I encourage you to take the time to read the entire story. It will help your understanding of the teaching here.

Joseph was the son of Jacob; he had eleven brothers. A psychologist will tell you that the more people living in a household, the more complicated the relationships and interactions. Take a piece of paper and draw a circle. Put a dot in the center to represent yourself. Now put dots on the outer part of the circle to represent other family members. Now draw a line from yourself to each other person, and draw a line from each dot on the outside of the circle to every other dot. The result will be a graphic representation of the relationships that exist in *your* household. See how complicated the situation was for Joseph and his brothers:

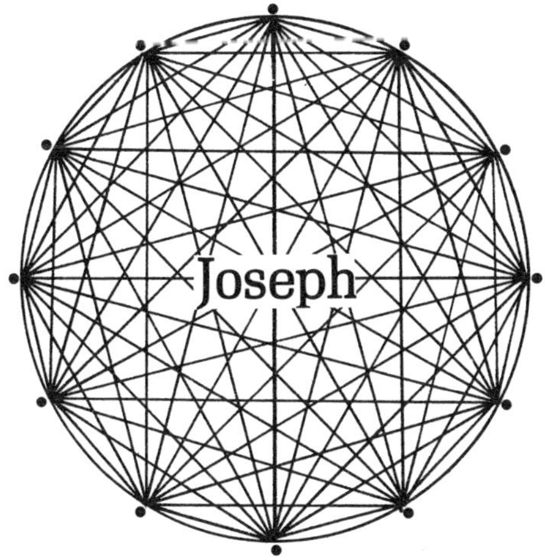

Joseph knew that he was special to God and that God had spoken to him through dreams (Genesis 37:5-11). He felt loved by his father, and he knew that he was his father's favorite. Furthermore, he didn't mind telling his brothers this. He was a little arrogant; yet God didn't remove the special call from Joseph. Jealousy filled Jacob's house! Have you ever been in this situation—knowing that you were a favorite child and feeling the jealousy of your brothers and sisters?

Perhaps that jealousy exists because you have been too bold in telling others that you are special. We must realize that it is *God* who places us in specific homes with specific parents for a special time and purpose we have on earth. That is not something to boast or complain about; it is something to keep in the quiet of our hearts as we continue in the work he calls us to do.

I often said to my children as they were growing up, "Dear, I didn't choose you to be a part of this family and you didn't choose us. But God somehow knew that our home would be the best environment for you in the first years of your life. This home is your beginning. We are responsible for your foundation—to teach you the Word and principles of God. Pray for us that we will be the parents God expects us to be."

One day Jacob sent Joseph on an errand (Genesis 37:13). He was to take food to his brothers who were tending their sheep in a far-off field. Joseph went willingly. Nothing appeared ominous about the day. It wasn't a special day on the calendar; Joseph didn't have a dream to warn him about this day. Very few of us have advance notice for the "big" days in our lives. Joseph had no opportunity to bid his father good-bye, take mementos with him, or appreciate the final exit from his home.

Joseph left home wearing a lovely handcrafted garment dyed with natural dyes from desert plants. This type of mantle or shawl takes years to make, and it often signifies a family inheritance in the Middle Eastern countries. When Joseph arrived at his brothers' camp, he was wearing the symbol of the very thing they hated: the fact that Jacob loved Joseph best.

The brothers plotted to kill Joseph. Reuben, his brother, stood up for him and talked the brothers into throwing Joseph into a nearby dry well. This is what they did—but not before they had stripped the garment from Joseph. The Bible tells us that Reuben intended to come back for Joseph (Genesis 37:22). Before he could do that, however, the other brothers had made a deal with a caravan of Ishmaelites. They sold Joseph as a slave.

Have you ever felt a situation was totally out of your control? Have you found yourself at the bottom of a dry, dark pit—put there by your own "brothers" or circumstances beyond your control? Have you found yourself set on a path—sold as a slave when you felt all the time you were a *chosen* child? The most important response is to realize this: if God has put his hand upon you, he will remain *in control* no matter what the circumstances. God protected Joseph, brought him out of the dark time, kept him alive, and stayed with him, even when Joseph was sold a second time (Genesis 37:36).

It is important to note that Joseph submitted his life to God's control. He did not allow bitterness or resentment to keep him from doing the best he could at whatever job was put before him. He did not allow his *spirit* to be enslaved. Colossians 3:23 advises us, "Whatever you do, do your work heartily, as for the Lord rather than for men."

Be aware that God is there with you at the bottom of the well. He is there with you as you ride the camel across the hot desert to a new land. He can turn even the most hopeless circumstance into a hope-filled experience. The Bible says that Christians should say as Paul said in Philippians 4:11, "I have learned to be content in whatever circumstances I am."

Joseph's story picks up again in Genesis 39. Joseph was sold in Egypt to the house of Potiphar, an Egyptian officer of Pharaoh. Potiphar was captain of the Pharaoh's bodyguard, and he had a large and prosperous house. Potiphar made Joseph the chief of all his servants. He was put in charge of all money and organization of the house. Joseph had surely been well prepared for the task—having lived in a home with eleven brothers! God had given Joseph the ability for the tasks he faced, and now he gave Joseph an *opportunity* to use and develop his abilities.

Then calamity struck again. Potiphar's wife decided that she wanted to have an affair with Joseph. She tempted Joseph repeatedly, and when Joseph rejected her and fled from her, she tore at his garment. Joseph escaped, but his outer garment stayed behind. In the wife's anger at not having her way with Joseph, she lied to Potiphar and said that *she* had refused the advances of Joseph and that Joseph had left his garment with her when she screamed. Have you ever been in a situation in which you were 100 percent right, but somehow others twisted the circumstances to make you appear 100 percent wrong? Well, Joseph found himself there!

It is important for us to recognize that Joseph didn't compromise himself with Potiphar's wife. He fled when he should have fled. He didn't stop to weigh the possible outcome. He could continue to stand totally pure and blameless before God. First Thessalonians 5:22 tells us to "abstain from every form of evil."

Nevertheless, Joseph was thrown into prison—yet another pit. Again, he didn't inwardly withdraw from the situation. Neither did he become a part of the filth and evilness of the prison. Joseph stayed true to his God even there.

At times you may find yourself in an evil situation. Take heart! The end to that situation will come. It may be school, your job, or a situation in your family or town. You may be tempted to withdraw from it or to participate fully in it. You don't need to do either. You can continue to love the Lord even in the midst of it. For example, if you find yourself in the midst of a situation where you feel sin is abounding, you could run from the situation or you could compromise yourself and participate in the sin. You don't need to do either. You can remain in the environment, but stay out of the sinful activity and love the Lord and radiate his love. That's what Joseph did.

And again, God delivered Joseph. Genesis 39:21 says, "But the Lord was with Joseph and extended kindness to him, and gave him favor in the sight of the chief jailor."

Joseph was in prison for two more years. It must have seemed much longer to him because he lived in the hope of release. He interpreted the dreams of a baker and a cupbearer, and saved the cupbearer's life in the process. Although the cupbearer had promised to put in a good word for Joseph with Pharaoh, "Yet the chief cupbearer did not remember Joseph, but forgot him" (Genesis 40:23).

Joseph lived daily with the expectation of getting out of prison, and every day he was disappointed. Do you live with that kind of expectation? It is important that you don't trade in your hope for bitterness. Believe that God is using this time for your good! See what happened to Joseph . . . .

Pharaoh had a dream. God could have caused Pharaoh to dream the day after the cupbearer's dream, but he didn't. God was using those two years to bring Joseph to full maturity and dependence upon him. And when Pharaoh had his dream, God also triggered the cupbearer's memory to recall that Joseph could interpret dreams. Joseph's situation changed dramatically and suddenly. Genesis 41:14 says:

Then Pharaoh sent and called for Joseph, and they hurriedly brought him out of the dungeon; and when he had shaved himself and changed his clothes, he came to Pharaoh.

Joseph found himself clean and clothed and standing before Pharaoh before he had time to realize what was happening. By the end of that day—having interpreted Pharaoh's dream correctly—Joseph was made prime minister of all the land. From prisoner to prime minister in one day—that's God's kind of promotion!

Joseph was given Pharaoh's signet ring, clothed in fine linen garments, and given a gold necklace. He rode in Pharaoh's chariot, saw the people bow to him, and was given authority over all the land of Egypt (Genesis 41:43). Pharaoh also gave Joseph a wife and made a decree that no man in Egypt should raise a hand or foot without Joseph's approval.

That day Joseph "graduated" from God's school. Betrayed by his brothers . . . thrown in a pit . . . enslaved in a foreign land . . . imprisoned for two years . . . Joseph's preparation suddenly came to fruition.

Can you put yourself in Joseph's shoes? What would you do if the responsibility for an entire nation fell into your lap? Perhaps a part of you would argue with God, saying, "Maybe I should only start with a fifth of the land, or half the land, to see how I do before I'm responsible for the entire country?" If God has called you to a special task that seems overwhelming to you—perhaps he is asking you to move to a different town, teach a class, or to do something that seems bigger than you are—you need to recognize that God doesn't call us to tasks for which we aren't prepared. If God has called you, he has equipped you and will continue to equip you to perform the task. All you have to do is obey, day by day by day by day. He expects you to depend on him, not on yourself.

Joseph ruled Egypt superbly. He had two sons. He prepared Egypt for a great famine. And the Bible says in Genesis 41:51 that Joseph came to the place in his life where he could say, "God has made me forget all my trouble. . . ."

As it turned out, Joseph was able to feed his brothers and father when famine hit the land. He held no bitterness against them. He could see how God had placed him in a position to *help* his family. In fact, if Joseph hadn't undergone the adversity, he could never have saved his family from a death by starvation and thereby fulfill his dreams.

Not only did Joseph feed his brothers and father, he prepared a land for them to live in. This was the land of Goshen, near Cairo. Jacob and his sons moved there, and the descendants of Jacob dwelt there for more than 400 years.

Joseph never went "home" again. He continued to live in Egypt, where he strengthened Pharaoh's holdings and governed the land with wisdom. He lived to see his great-great-grandchildren living in Egypt. You, too, may not end up at the place you began. You may be looking back, hoping to go "home" again. That may not be God's plan for you. God may have all the *riches* of life—the blessings and sense of purpose—still ahead for you.

When we look at Joseph's life as a whole, we see a man who had constant, and sometimes difficult, changes in his life. Yet two truths stand out clearly: *Joseph was totally committed to God.* He never forsook God. He made the best of every situation in which he found himself. He found work to do and kept his sense of purpose no matter how dark the circumstances. He believed that God would prevail for him.

Second, *God never forsook Joseph.* He honored Joseph's obedience. He fulfilled his call on Joseph's life. He brought Joseph into a place of honor, authority, blessing, and responsibility.

When situations in our life get dark, we need to follow Joseph's example: remain true to God, believe that God will remain true to us, and continue to walk on, one foot up and one foot down, knowing that no situation stays the same or is without a divine purpose.

Have you ever stopped to think of the earthly life of our Lord Jesus Christ as a journey? In Jesus' life on this planet he experienced every emotion and every difficulty you or I will ever face. He walked the road we walk.

Jesus was born in a manger. Can any birth be as lowly or as humiliating as being born in a barn?

He was born in a very small town that was overrun with teeming crowds gathered for a tax census. Can any birth be more obscure or go less noticed by the masses?

He was born to a virgin, a young woman. Can anyone be more inexperienced as a mother?

As a young boy, Jesus was uprooted from his homeland and sent across a desert into a foreign country. He literally ran for his life. He ended up in a ghetto, surrounded by strange sights and sounds and people who spoke a different language. Can any early childhood be filled with more trauma and fear?

He grew up in Nazareth, where people didn't understand his virgin birth. Can any young person undergo more ridicule?

When Jesus was twelve, he and his family went to Jerusalem. His parents left for the return trip home without him, and didn't even realize he was missing for three days. Can any small-town youth feel more forgotten or more left alone in a large city? Can any person feel a greater sense of abandonment? Of course, until Jesus' parents found him he was content to remain in the Temple. But although he was very God, Jesus was also very man, and he must have felt abandoned.

He lived in obscurity for many years, toiling with his hands at menial labor. Could any life be more monotonous and apparently meaningless?

At thirty, he was baptized in the Jordan River and anointed for his special mission on earth. He began to teach the people and perform miracles. He cured the demon-possessed and the leprous and forgave the sins of the lowliest people in the land. Could any person walk a more austere road of ministry?

His apostles saw him walk on water, heal the lame, and calm the storms. They heard him preach to the masses, saw him feed the multitudes, raise a man from the dead, and overturn the money tables in the Temple. Yet even these devoted followers—his best friends—denied they knew him when the going got rough. Could any person be more rejected by his friends?

Jesus felt the total, complete rejection of God, too. He felt emotion, pain, anguish, hurt. He bore all of the psychological distress we feel as he prayed in the Garden of Gethsemane. He bore this grief *alone.*

He lived a life without sin, and yet he was beaten that we might be healed. He was nailed to a cross to die for the sins of all mankind. He died the most abhorrent death of his age. He was buried in another man's tomb. Could any person be wronged more completely or die with any less dignity and estate?

And yet . . .

Jesus is enthroned today as the King of the Universe. He arose from the dead! He was seen alive and walking on the earth by hundreds of people after his death by crucifixion. He ascended into the heavens. And today he is sitting at the right hand of God. He receives the constant adoration of the hosts of heaven. He has all riches, authority, and power at his fingertips—all the *universe* bows in his honor and follows his commands!

When we look at Jesus' journey on earth, we have no excuse for giving in to our circumstances. We all have cause to hope. We all have reason to believe that we, too, shall rise and reign with God one day. Because he did, we will too.

Joseph lived many years. His rewards were great on earth. His rewards were visible to many. Jesus lived only a few years on earth. His rewards were, in many instances, only visible to himself. He did not make the headlines of his day as Joseph did. He *knew,* however, that he was doing the Father's will, and that was satisfying to him. Jesus' greatest rewards and victories came through his death and resurrection. He is alive today—and the rewards continue to mount in his favor. As we live our lives for his sake, *we* are his reward.

Our lives may not pattern the journey of either Joseph or Jesus. And yet we can learn from both. God rewards those who love him and are obedient to his call. Some receive their rewards on earth . . . others in the resurrection . . . others in both! God *ultimately* gives joy and purpose and honor to those who remain faithful to him. That is confirmed in promise after promise, journey after journey in the Bible.

And we know that, as in the lives of Joseph and Jesus, situations do change. Life moves on. Time ticks by. Every low is matched by a *greater high* in God's plan.

You may not be able to see your way clear if you are in a difficult situation today. That's the best time I know to do a journey study of your own. That's the best time to go back and read about Joseph, or read and reread the Gospel of Mark. Or you may want to follow the journeys of these men and women:

Jonah—see the Book of Jonah
Ruth—see the Book of Ruth
The children of Israel as they left Egypt—see Exodus
David—see 1 Samuel
Paul—see Acts 7, 13—28

Journey studies ultimately teach us that God has a plan for each of our lives. God wants us to be obedient to him. He is working all the time—even when we sleep—for our ultimate good. He can turn every darkness into shining day.

Journey studies will show you the purpose for your life, give you hope, and help you believe in the goodness of God.

Journey studies will help you see that life has an eternal destination, far beyond the circumstances and situations of this life.

Journey studies will help you see your own life in new perspective—that, as a child of God, you are destined to be a priest and king of this world! You are destined for great rewards throughout eternity!

DOES IT REALLY WORK?

Are you asking yourself that question, or perhaps other questions such as these:

It sounds wonderful, but can I do it?
Am I disciplined enough to stick with daily Bible reading?
Am I spiritual enough to understand passages for myself?

Or perhaps you have practical questions, such as:

How long will it take before I am ready for subject studies?
How can I get my husband or wife and children interested in studying the Bible with me?
How long before I feel a consistent growth in my understanding of the Bible?

Let me share with you some of the experiences of my friends.

Trish and Brett were jet-setters. They had a very successful business and led an active social life, surrounding themselves with what they felt were the best people and the best things in the best places of the world. Brett felt he had been a Christian all his life. Trish, on the other hand, felt she had never truly known the Lord. She also felt that if she just could understand the Bible, she would have answers for her life. At cocktail parties, she would ask people, "Do *you* understand the Bible?

Trish and Brett went to many churches, searching for socialites like themselves who might be able to read and understand the Bible. Finally Brett gave up the search. At that, Trish panicked.

She accepted an invitation to attend a luncheon at a church in her neighborhood, and while there she heard a woman speak on a topic that interested her: "How to Be a Good Wife and Mother." She called the speaker the next day to find out where she could learn more about the Bible for herself, and soon she was an active part of our Bible study. Both she and her husband made decisions to follow Jesus as their personal Lord and to read the Bible daily.

They bought a Bible at a local department store and put it on their dining table. They would read aloud to each other every morning. After two weeks, they were frustrated. They felt by then they should have had all the answers to their questions and problems! Instead, they found many of the passages confusing. We encouraged them to keep going, and they did. In spite of their frustration at times, they found themselves enticed by the practical ideas they found in the Bible.

Trish and Brett invested in other versions and copies of the Bible, and eventually they had a Bible in every room of their home—including each bathroom—as well as a Bible in each car and one at Brett's office. Whenever they sat down for a few minutes, they'd pick up a Bible.

Beyond their reading, they began to discuss the Bible with each other. They'd meet for lunch and talk about the Bible. They'd drive together to a meeting and talk about the Bible. They'd ask each other:

What did you read today?
What did it mean to you?
What did you pray about today?
What answers to prayer did you receive today?
What has God done for you today?

Trish and Brett had led a social life that revolved around drinking. One day they asked us, "Will God let us drink?" We told them that the Bible had many references to this, and we encouraged them to check out the answer for themselves by doing a word study on strong drink. They did, and in the process they discovered they could look up *any* question in their lives and do word studies to find the answers.

When Brett faced business decisions, he'd look up "money" or "business" and do word studies on them. These studies led him into a thorough study on finance. Brett found it difficult to tell his employees—all women—about his relationship with the Lord, so he gave them an extra coffee break every day to listen to a fifteen-minute women's radio program about the Bible. Within two weeks, all of the women in his office had made personal decisions to accept Jesus as Lord of their lives. Brett and his staff now have a weekly Bible study staff meeting!

Trish turned to the Bible for direction about being a good mother, and she found the direction she needed through subject studies on children and marriage. Today, their children have well-balanced lives and each one has a deep love for Jesus.

Together, Brett and Trish did a journey study on Paul—and what a blessing to them as a couple when they looked back on the journeys of their own lives and saw the hand of God at work in their lives even before they had made personal commitments to him.

Within a year, their entire family was conversing about the Bible. The children felt very close to their parents because they were included in Bible discussions. Their love for Jesus deepened beyond anything they could have imagined. They would often say to us, "When you know the Author of the Bible, it's not difficult to be obedient to whatever he tells you to do!" Best of all, Trish and Brett knew that no matter what problems they faced, they could find the solutions in the Bible. They knew God would give them the strength to put the Bible to work in their lives.

By the way, Trish and Brett didn't stop jet-setting

around the world, but their reason for travel changed. (They now visit missions.)

They didn't stop socializing, but their company changed. (They now entertain fellow-believers.)

Their enthusiasm for life didn't diminish; in fact, they have more enthusiasm than ever before!

Carolyn was brought into Bible study by a different need in her life. She and her husband loved each other greatly, but their marriage was difficult for Carolyn in many ways. Her husband demanded a great deal of her, including an edict that she stay at home and not be part of outside groups or activities. Carolyn felt very confused about what a wife should—or should not—be.

One day she came to our Bible class and learned that she could look up answers to her specific questions in the Bible.

Almost immediately, Carolyn became especially fond of journey studies. She followed the lives of Hannah, Miriam, and Eve, and although these women's lives were very different from her own, they showed her that God could deal with individuals in unique and exciting ways.

Carolyn decided to try Bible study for a year, to do exactly what she felt the Bible was telling her to do, and to trust God for the right attitude toward her husband and herself.

A great peace filled her home as a result of her Bible study and her decision to put the Bible into practical application in her life and home. Her husband sensed this great peace; he eased his demands and allowed Carolyn to volunteer her abilities to a women's ministry on a part-time basis.

And then Carolyn's husband was critically injured in an automobile accident as he drove to work one morning. As Carolyn sat by his bedside while he was in a coma, she realized how much she had learned from the Bible and how much she relied on it for strength in her daily life. She faced the possibility of her husband's death squarely—doing word studies on healing, resurrection, death, faith, hope, and eternal life. She discussed these studies with her friends. She felt herself growing stronger instead of weaker as the days passed.

Carolyn's husband died about a week after his accident, and her continued reliance upon the Word of God allowed her a great peace during that difficult time. She had loved her husband deeply, and she felt the loss of his presence deeply; and yet the love of God, made evident to her through the Bible and her Christian friends, was deeper still. Today Carolyn and her two young daughters have placed their total security in Jesus. They talk about the Bible among themselves as a routine matter. They have a fulfillment that is abiding.

When Laura came to know Jesus as her personal Lord, she began to read the Bible in Matthew as we suggested. She was fascinated by all she read. And then she began to read Mark. She thought to herself, "This is all the same. I've read these stories before." She thumbed through her Bible to Luke and John, and was soon convinced that all of the books of the Bible were the same—just different versions of the same stories. So she put her Bible aside.

Not long after that, a friend called Laura. In the course of their conversation, Laura told her friend about her newfound relationship with Jesus. Laura's friend was a bit aghast and warned Laura about becoming a religious fanatic. "I surely hope you don't end up believing that God can heal you any time you have the slightest ailment, or begin to speak in tongues or pray in public like some people I hear about!"

Rather than be discouraged at this warning, Laura was intrigued. She hadn't read much in Matthew about God's healing people today, or about praying in public or speaking in tongues. She took her Bible out by the pool and during a long afternoon of sunbathing and swimming did word studies that spilled over into subject studies in all three areas. She read for hours about the Holy Spirit, healing, and prayer. Not only did she learn a great deal about the principles of God, she learned there was more—much more—to the Bible than the Gospels.

A few months later, her son Mark was injured while

playing basketball. He was the star of his high-school team, and by all appearances his arm was broken, which would mean he was out for the rest of the season.

While sitting with her son in the emergency room at the hospital, Laura took charge. "Why be in a cast when Jesus can heal you?" she asked Mark. Then she began to look through the cabinets in the room for some oil. (She had read in her study on healing about anointing the sick with oil. She hadn't remembered, however, that the passage referred to the elders of the church!) Mark suggested they wait until after the X-rays were taken, so they'd know the full extent of his injury. Sure enough, he had a fractured arm.

While waiting for the doctor to return to set the bone and cast the arm, Laura and Mark began to pray. "You have to believe with me," she told Mark. "The Bible says two or more have to agree together." So they prayed aloud and believed together.

When the doctor returned, they asked if it was possible for Mark's arm to be put in something other than plaster. Rather reluctantly, the doctor agreed to wrap the arm in a flexible Ace bandage.

Within two weeks, Mark felt a new strength in his arm and asked to be allowed to play basketball again. A second X-ray was taken—and the arm was healed! Mark continued to play throughout the season, without injury, further mishap, or any pain. The healing had occurred in miracle time!

Later, through this incident, Mark's coach accepted Jesus into his life as his personal Lord. What a marvelous faith-building series of incidents in all of their lives! The Lord truly rewarded Laura's faith and the prayers of her friends. Laura had discovered that the Bible was indeed practical and applicable to her everyday circumstances—all because a word study had prompted her to explore new areas of God's Word.

Susanne had a great difficulty with Bible reading on two accounts. First, reading was difficult for her. It took her a great deal of time to read even a chapter. Second, she wasn't a very disciplined person, especially in attending Bible studies. She decided to confront both weaknesses in her life in a straightforward manner. She offered to hold a Bible study in her home—and that meant she *had* to attend!

Next, she asked for a specific Christmas present: the Bible on cassette tapes. That way she could *listen* to the Word of God as she went about her daily chores and leisure activities. She added a variety of Bible study tapes to her "listening library," and she made it a habit to keep the television set in her home tuned to a Christian channel. The Word of God filled her home and became a part of her life, through her sense of hearing more than her sense of sight. Her control of the television and tape recorder was a great facet in her ministry to her family, too!

Bill also found that cassette tapes were a fine means of taking the Bible into his life. He'd listen to them on the way to work. And when he took his boys on fishing trips, they'd listen to the Bible tapes all the way to the lake. They'd discuss what they heard throughout the day, and then if they had questions they'd listen again to the tapes on the way home. If they still had questions, they'd write them down and look up the answers as soon as they got home. In that way, father and sons all became thoroughly familiar with the Word.

When Bill began to study Proverbs, he discovered a gold mine of practical advice on how to be a good father. He'd gather his family around the coffee table in their living room and pray and read aloud to them from Proverbs with great boldness—sometimes to the amusement of the boys, but always to the enrichment of the family. In these ways, the Bible became a family affair and a daily part of their lives as they together explored God's plan for them.

Margo and Scott were a very sophisticated and wealthy couple. They divorced after twenty-one years of marriage and five children. Their marriage had been laden with a multitude of problems. Now both divorcees were miserable.

Scott came to a personal relationship with Jesus while at a business appointment with a member of our Bible study group. Soon after, he and Margo were invited to a dinner party with a group of believers, and Margo made a decision to accept Jesus as the Lord of her life. Although excited about their newfound faith, and also a newfound love for each other, neither Margo nor Scott knew how to read the Bible for themselves. They began to read the Bible with childlike faith, taking the practical straightforward suggestions of the Bible at face value. They'd often call an "older" member of the Bible study group to ask, "Is that right?" This was especially important for Scott, who in his enthusiasm had a tendency to read individual Scriptures out of context.

Over the months, their relationship began to be reconciled, and after three years of divorce they were remarried. They attended a couples' retreat. There, they confronted a Scripture that made them realize that although they had experienced forgiveness from God, they had not forgiven each other. That night they confessed many of their faults to each other in writing, talked about their faults, and asked forgiveness of each other. They then burned the papers on which they had identified their sins, and together they cast the ashes into the ocean.

Margo and Scott continued to rely upon the Bible for specific direction in working out their reconciliation. Margo, for example, had accepted a ring from a boyfriend while she was divorced. She was obstinate in her desire to keep the ring after her remarriage to Scott, although the ring was offensive to him. Margo asked advice from a member of the Bible study group, and she suggested that Margo do a word study on "ring." Margo was *glad* to return the ring when she saw what it represented!

Scott began to realize that his business had kept him from his family, and as he read in the Bible about how God would have a man conduct business, he realized that he could no longer operate as he once had. He began to divest himself of his interests and to spend more time with his wife and children, taking them on mission trips and to

Israel. (Scott wanted his entire family to be able to visualize the places they read about in the Bible.)

Margo and Scott discovered that they really couldn't study the Bible together. They read at different paces and had different study interests. But several times a week they would gather the children together and read the Bible as a family. The children, who had suffered greatly through the years of divorce, began to experience individual healings as the spiritual climate in the home changed.

Scott was so convinced that the Bible had changed his life that he invested in Bibles bound with olive wood to have available in his office. He gave the Bibles to clients and friends along with a stern admonition, "I'm only giving you this Bible if you'll read it. If you read it, it will change your life. But if you aren't going to read it, then give it back, because I want my Bibles to be put into the hands of people who will use them!" Scott has given away several hundred Bibles in recent years, claiming a new believer before God for each one.

I can think of dozens of other real-life incidents to share with you, but I hope you are able to tell from these few examples that every person's approach to Bible study varies.

Each person brings to Bible study unique needs and experiences.
Each person devises his or her own way of including family members in Bible study.
Each person finds his own spiritual life deepening at a different rate.

You may move almost immediately into subject and journey studies once you become familiar with a concordance. You may find word studies so intriguing that you will limit yourself to them for several weeks or months. There's no set formula. No matter the pace of your growth and understanding, you will always want to do word studies. You will *add* subject studies and journey studies in a natural way as you grow spiritually and become more confident that the Bible really *can* meet needs in your life.

Many of our friends have taken the "I'll try it for a year" approach, figuring that they'll put the Bible to the test and then take stock of their lives and their ability to understand the Bible. Actually, this is a fine approach and I recommend it heartily—in part, because I don't know a single person who has done this diligently and then has given up his study of the Bible!

There's really only one way you're going to find out if the Bible can work for you, if you are disciplined enough for daily reading, or if you're capable of understanding the Bible for yourself. And that is to *try it*—to get started with five-minute readings and progress as your curiosity and life's situations prompt you to ask questions and seek the Bible's answers. The Bible can be applied to your life by one person only . . . and that's *you!*

BOOK II

THE KEY TO DEEPER UNDERSTANDING

Have you ever stopped to think about the great power of *spoken* language?

Our tongues can be our worst enemies or our best friends. The Bible tells us in James 3 that the tongue is the most unruly member of the body. Very often, we are able to discipline just about every area of our lives *except* what we say.

On the other hand, the Bible also refers to the great *power* resident in the spoken word. The "foolishness of preaching," as Paul calls it in 1 Corinthians 1:23, has been used effectively for God's purposes. Faith comes through hearing the spoken word of God (Romans 10:17).

The power of the spoken word extends to prayer. Many promises related to prayer include the phrase "whatever we ask." Not think . . . *ask*. In praying audibly we are giving notice to the universe that we are requesting power for our lives from Almighty God. We are heard by the powers of both heaven and earth. It is as if we are writing out a purchase order of our needs and requests, and signing it over to the charge account of Jesus. Jesus signs the bottom line and hands the request on to the Father.

When we pray aloud, we can expect action. The Bible says that Daniel prayed three times a day and "gave thanks" (Daniel 6:10)—and he prayed loudly enough that he was heard and thrown into the lion's den for it! (In order, of course, that his witness might be a dramatic one to the king and the people of his land.) In Acts 16:25 we read how Paul and Silas prayed and sang praises before the earthquake that led to their release from prison!

Prayer is your most powerful help in reading and studying the Bible.

As you read, look for prayers. Circle them in your Bible. Note that the people are often praying *aloud*, and they are either thanking God for something or asking him for something. Very often they are thanking God first and then asking. Their prayers have direct purposes. For example:

See Hannah's prayer in 1 Samuel 1:10, 11. She prayed and wept before God, asking him for a son and promising to give that son back to God. See 1 Samuel 2:1-10 where Hannah *thanked* God for giving her a son—and where she in turn kept her promise and gave Samuel to Eli, the priest, for God's service.

See Hezekiah's prayer (2 Kings 19:15-19) in which he presented his case to God in clear-cut terms—telling God about his enemies and being specific about what he wanted God to do to them. See how clearly he expressed his claims and requests. See also his declaration of thanks, voicing aloud that God was Maker and Ruler of heaven and earth.

See the prayer of Jesus at Lazarus' tomb in John 11:41, 42. He prayed, "Father, I thank thee that thou hast heard me. And I knew that thou hearest me always: but because of the people which stand by I said it, that they may believe that thou hast sent me." And then He called, "Lazarus come forth!"

It is the *praises* to God that we can keep in our hearts—turning our minds and emotions over to praise in the still quiet of our inner persons. We are to live in an attitude of praise around the clock, either audibly or silently. Our prayers of thanksgiving and of request, however, are usually *voiced*.

Lynn and Richard are two of my favorite friends. They have a wonderful marriage. A few years ago, they each hoped for "something better" in the life of the other.

Lynn knew that Richard was a believer, but she had never heard him pray aloud or express his faith. She longed to pray with her husband and discuss the Bible with him. It seemed to her that they could talk about everything *but* the Bible. In that area, a barrier of silence separated them.

Richard knew that Lynn was in good health, but he wanted her to be even stronger and more limber. He believed she'd feel better if she'd jog with him every morning.

So they made a pact. Lynn agreed to get up at 6 A.M. every day to jog around a neighborhood track with Richard, if Richard would pray aloud with her as they jogged. (She had read that a good jogging pace was one during which a person could carry on a conversation without gasping!)

And it worked. Their plan opened up a new area of communication between them. Lynn feels better physically; Richard feels better spiritually. And they have become closer to each other.

When you pray, pray in Jesus' name. The Bible tells us that every power in heaven and in earth is under the name of Jesus. There are many powers on earth, but Jesus' name has power in *heaven* and earth. In ancient days, servants conducted business in the name of their masters. In like manner, Jesus' name carries all the authority we need in approaching God. We are given the same consideration in heaven that Jesus is given when we come in his name.

When you pray, don't memorize your prayers or get into a habit of only reading prayers. The prayers in the Bible and the prayers on the previous pages of this book are meant as guidelines for you. They are a good beginning point in opening your conversation with God. They are not intended as an end unto themselves. Make these prayers your own and add to them. Don't be afraid of being creative in your prayers.

Actually, prayer is the most intimate form of communication you will ever know. It is talking with your best friend, your Friend of friends. Just as with human friends, you'll want to stay on "speaking terms" with God. You don't communicate in pious, lofty tones with your friends or use unfamiliar "thees" and "thous." Rather, you use everyday language and everyday rhythms of speaking. This is also the way to communicate with God.

Tell God:

what you like and dislike about a situation
how you feel—what hurts, where and why you think it hurts
what you need and why you have this need.

When you pray before you study the Bible, deal in specifics. Ask for:

insight . . . *that you might see new meanings with clarity and precision in a specific passage. Ask, "What does this mean, Lord?"*
personal application . . . *that you might see definite and specific practical ways for the passage to come alive in your life. Ask, "What does this have to do with me, Jesus?"*
synthesis . . . *that you might remember other passages that relate to your present study. Ask, "How does this fit into the whole of the Bible?"*
concentration . . . *that you might not be distracted by everyday trivia as you delve into these extended studies. "Please help me, Lord, to contemplate solely on your Word."*

Above all, ask for the guidance and presence of the Holy Spirit as your Teacher of the Bible.

The Bible says in Ephesians 1:17, "I keep asking that the God of our Lord Jesus Christ, the glorious Father, may give you the Spirit of wisdom and revelation, so that you may know him better" *(New International Version). The Holy Spirit is vital* to your personal application of the Bible.

I invite you to do a summary study on the Holy Spirit by first doing a word study, then a subject study, and then a journey study on this third person of the Trinity.

THE HOLY SPIRIT IN WORD STUDY

Look up *Spirit, Holy Spirit,* or *Holy Ghost.* Two of my favorite references are Zechariah 4:6 (which says that happenings in our world occur not by might, nor by power, but by the Spirit of the Lord) and Luke 11:13 (which promises that the Father will give his Holy Spirit to all who ask).

Also in doing a word study, you may look up *Spirit of truth.* Three very special references are found in the middle of the Gospel of John: John 14:16, 17 (which says that the Spirit of truth will dwell in those who receive him); John 15:26 (which explains that the Spirit of truth comes from God the Father and testifies about Jesus); John 16:13-15 (which promises that the Spirit of truth is our ultimate teacher).

You'll find other references that speak directly to you.

THE HOLY SPIRIT IN SUBJECT STUDY

Word studies tell us who the Holy Spirit is, and a subject study on the Holy Spirit elaborates on how the Holy Spirit works in our lives.

Look up the *fruits* of the Holy Spirit in Galatians 5, especially verses 5, 16, 22, 23, and 25. That chapter of Galatians also points out the opposites to the fruits of the Spirit.

Look up the *gifts* of the Holy Spirit in 1 Corinthians 12.

You may want to devise an organization chart to see the relationship of the Holy Spirit to other heavenly, and earthly, beings. Here's a beginning:

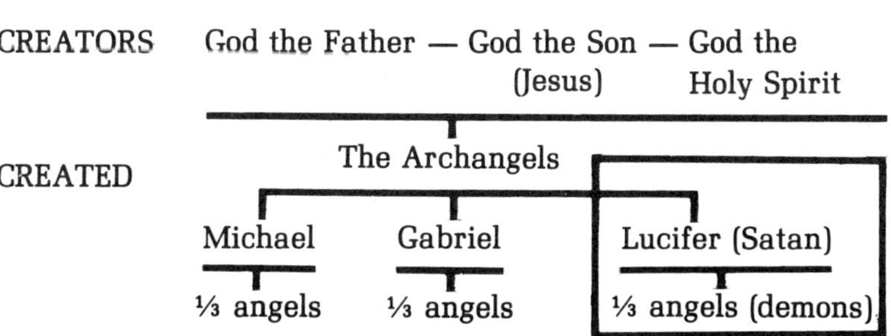

You will note that Lucifer is not the opposite of Jesus. He's *below* the authority of Christ. Evil spirits, such as mentioned in Matthew 12:28, are not opposite to the Holy Spirit. They are far *below* the Holy Spirit. This explains our authority in the Holy Spirit to have dominion over evil powers.

Look up verses related to the *character* of the Holy Spirit. In Acts 2, he is the promise of the Father fulfilled in our lives. In 1 Corinthians 12—14, he does not behave unseemly, but is the author of order. In John 14:26, Jesus refers to the Holy Spirit as our Comforter. Romans 8:2 promises us that the Holy Spirit will set us free from sin and death—he is the Spirit of resurrection. And later, in Romans 8:26, we are told that the Holy Spirit helps us when we are weak.

THE HOLY SPIRIT IN JOURNEY STUDY

The Holy Spirit came and went from the earth until the Day of Pentecost, which was forty days after Jesus was crucified. The Bible foretold in Genesis 6:3 that the Spirit of the Lord would not always strive with man, and this was true for centuries.

Genesis 1:2 says that the Spirit of God moved upon the waters and was the force behind all of creation. But then, throughout the Old Testament, the Holy Spirit came and went from the earth. He revealed himself in special ways to individuals who were given specific tasks and abilities.

In Judges 14:6, the Holy Spirit came to Samson as his Protector and enabled him to tear apart with his bare hands a young lion that roared against him, using no weapons.

The Holy Spirit gave Gideon authority to gather an army, wisdom to determine God's timing through a fleece, faith to trust God for a victory with only 300 soldiers, courage to obey God and use a pitcher, trumpet, and light instead of swords in doing battle. (See Judges 6:34.)

In 1 Samuel 11:6, 7, Saul was given a simple plan by the Holy Spirit that brought the Israelites to a place where they revered God more than they feared their enemies.

Through this, Saul was crowned king of the nation.

In 1 Samuel 16:13, David received a special and lasting anointing from Samuel in the presence of his older brothers. That anointing of the Holy Spirit stayed with him all his life—through good days and bad, friends and enemies—until he became King of Israel.

In Judges 3:10 the Holy Spirit gave Othniel, not a well-known Bible hero, the ability to lead the Israelites into war against the Babylonians, their slave masters. They then lived in freedom for forty years.

In 2 Chronicles 24:20, the Holy Spirit came to Zechariah, the priest, who then called his people to repentance. The Holy Spirit gave him the power to stand by his message, even though the people stoned him to death.

The Holy Spirit descended upon Jesus like a dove, as we read in Matthew 3:16. This was the anointing that began Jesus' ministry on earth.

Jesus said to his followers in John 16:7, 8 that he was leaving the earth, but that they weren't to be dismayed. The Holy Spirit would take up residency on earth in his place, covering the whole earth with his presence at the same time. Jesus promised that the Holy Spirit would be their Comforter, convict the world of sin, lead men to righteousness, and execute judgment.

And in Acts 2 we read that the Holy Spirit came to earth to take up residency in the lives of the believers, filling each of them with a type of personal power not known before in the history of man. The Holy Spirit continues to reside on the earth. That is why, today, we have more understanding of the Word of God than ever before. More people on earth are filled with the Spirit of God than at any other time (Ephesians 3:5).

At the end of the age, the Holy Spirit and the believers will invite Jesus back to the earth to establish his reign (Revelation 22:17). Jesus is waiting for this invitation: "Come, Lord Jesus, come quickly."

As you read and study about the Holy Spirit, I believe one truth will become clear to you: the Holy Spirit is your ultimate Bible Teacher. In fact, you cannot begin to understand the *deep* truths of the Bible unless the Holy Spirit reveals them to you. And prayer is the *way* you place yourself in a position of total dependence and reliance upon the Holy Spirit to teach you the truth of God's Word. Prayer is the key to unlocking the deep spiritual truths of the Bible.

PROGRESSION STUDIES

When you were a child—or perhaps when your children were young—did you have a growth chart somewhere in your home? A notched doorjamb or a marked wall or a tape-measure strip on the inside of the closet door? We did. And every month or so the children would want to take a measurement to see if, and how much, they had grown. Children expect to grow! They just don't realize how fast it will happen.

One of the great principles of life is *growth*. Everything around us is either growing or decaying. Life has stages—ups and downs—but the overall thrust of our Christian life is growth. We always have room to become more than we are today. Our potential in Christ is unlimited.

Journey studies lead us to the understanding that life is in constant motion. Situations change. People change. Attitudes and opinions of men change. Journey studies call us to see that our *natural* life has a progression to it.

In progression studies we are concerned with progress in our *spiritual* lives. The Christian life must have an *upward* trend so that we are always growing more into the likeness of Christ, closer to God, and upward in spirit

*Scripture references in this chapter are taken from the *New International Version*.

to heaven. We are to be like a business chart that shows a constant rise in profits year after year after year. Progression studies lead us to an awareness that we build our lives experience upon experience and understanding upon understanding.

Ephesians 4:15 says we are to "grow up into him, who is the Head, that is, Christ."

We are told in 1 Peter 2:2 that we are to long for spiritual milk, that by it we may "grow up in your salvation." And in 2 Peter 3:18 we are encouraged to "grow in the grace and knowledge of our Lord and Savior Jesus Christ."

Our lives are to unfold, develop, grow, progress.

Several passages of Scripture can also be viewed as *progressions.* These passages—or verses within a passage—have a relationship with one another. One verse is based on the foundation laid by the previous verse. One chapter builds upon another chapter. One book of the Bible uses another book as a stepping-stone to understanding.

Some very familiar passages of Scripture may be read in a *progressive* way. I would like to say at the beginning of our study that this is not the *only* way in which these passages may be read. One of the wonderful characteristics of the Bible is that it can be interpreted on many different levels. A passage might be read on the *physical* level, with the truths applied directly to everyday, practical situations in life. This same passage may be read on a *spiritual* level, with the same truths applied to the growth of a person's relationship with Christ.

The best way to really describe a progression study is to do one. So let's take one of the most obvious, which is also one of the most familiar passages in all the Bible. It is found in Matthew 5:3-12. This is the Beatitude portion of the Sermon on the Mount.

Blessed are the poor in spirit, for theirs is the kingdom of heaven.

Blessed are those who mourn, for they will be comforted.

Blessed are the meek, for they will inherit the earth.

Blessed are those who hunger and thirst for righteousness, for they will be filled.
Blessed are the merciful, for they will be shown mercy.
Blessed are the pure in heart, for they will see God.
Blessed are the peacemakers, for they will be called sons of God.
Blessed are those who are persecuted because of righteousness, for theirs is the kingdom of heaven.
Blessed are you when people insult you, persecute you and falsely say all kinds of evil against you because of me. Rejoice and be glad, because great is your reward in heaven, for in the same way they persecuted the prophets who were before you.

In taking a passage of Scripture for a progression study, it's a good idea to read the *entire* passage first to gain a sense of the whole. Then you can go back to the first verse and begin your in-depth study.

This passage may be regarded as a ladder of spiritual growth. Each verse is like a rung on a ladder. This passage describes a progression that each of us goes through as we follow Christ and grow in our relationship with him.

Beginning with Matthew 5:3 . . .

Blessed are the poor in spirit. . . . What does it mean to be poor in spirit? Basically it means that we recognize that our human spirit is not enough. When somebody is called poor in material goods, it means that other people are recognized as wealthy. Poor is a *contrast* only to wealth. One of our presidents once said, "When I was growing up I was poor, but I didn't know it." Many people in our world are spiritually poor—they just don't know it. They haven't met anyone yet who is spiritually rich!

RICH, BUT POOR

Anne was raised in a poor home, but married into great wealth. She loved her husband greatly and had the son she had always wanted. As much as she enjoyed the wealth in her life, she found that she was bankrupt in her soul. She felt the same poverty in her inner life that she had known materially as a child. When her hairdresser brought her to a Bible study, she immediately recognized her need . . . and the solution to it. She began to devour the Word of God, and her entire family now knows the Lord. They have become rich in their *spirits.*

Irv was president of his country club. He was proud of his socialite wife, his golf trophies, and his very successful business. One day he awoke to find that his wife was planning to leave him, a physical injury was going to keep him from the golf course, and his business associate was taking another job. He *knew* the poverty in his spirit that day. He knew he had to make decisions that would restore his soul. He accepted Jesus as his Lord, and this led to his being reunited with his wife. He sold his business. And he found a new love to replace golf: night classes in a Bible school!

None of us begins to grow in Christ until we admit that we don't know it all and that there is more of the spiritual realm of life to gain. Our experience often begins when we meet a person who is so filled with the Holy Spirit of God that we are forced to say, "I've met someone who has a full dose of God's Spirit! I'm really poor by comparison. I only have my *own* spirit. I don't have God's Spirit in me." We cry out to Jesus for his Spirit to live within us. (This comes with the born-again experience.) And Jesus promises us that our cry for salvation will be heard. The reward is clearly stated: . . . *for theirs is the kingdom of heaven.*

The next verse describes the next stage in our spiritual quest. *Blessed are those who mourn. . . .* The very first thing that happens to you when you are born of the Spirit and begin to grow in Christ is that you mourn within your heart for all those you love who haven't yet made this decision. If you are going to heaven and you know it, you won't be satisfied to go alone! You'll want everybody you love to make the journey with you. You'll grieve in your spirit until your loved ones make a decision for Christ. God says: . . . *they will be comforted.* A promise to us is found in Psalm 126:6:

He who goes out weeping, carrying seed to sow, will return with songs of joy, carrying sheaves with him.

THE MOURNERS

Karyn's acceptance of Jesus totally revolutionized her life. She went immediately into word studies about heaven to discover *when* she could see Jesus. Her love for Jesus was the *all* of her life. She began to pray and weep for her widowed mother to love Jesus as she did. But when she tried to tell her mother about her love for Jesus, she couldn't seem to find the words. Karyn's way of sharing her love for the Lord with her mother was to tell her about heaven and about seeing Jesus someday.

What was in Karyn's life was so obviously good and right that her mother made a special effort to thank those who had given Karyn a Bible. The day soon came when she wanted this relationship for herself. She, in turn, shared her love for the Lord with all her neighbors. Not long after that, Karyn's mother died, and her eyes then saw "the glory of the coming of the Lord."

The next Beatitude says: *Blessed are the meek. . . .* Many of us become so excited about our new lives in Christ that we aren't too meek at times. We're so eager to tell everyone about the changes he has made in our lives that we appear proud and "better-than-thou." Jesus tells us we need to be gentle and humble. We are to please Jesus and not try to please everyone else.

You don't have to prove yourself to anyone. You don't have you tell anybody how good you are, what you've accomplished, or defend yourself. You don't have to lose your temper with those who don't recognize your life in Christ. You just have to stand totally open and meek before God. When you get to this place, God will know that he can trust you with responsibilities in his work. God's master plan is for his children to rule this earth someday! Only as you become meek will God be able to trust you to reign as a king and priest of this earth with justice and compassion. The Beatitude concludes . . . *for they will inherit the earth.*

Have you found your rung on the ladder of spiritual growth yet? If so, this is the area on which you are to concentrate at this time. God wants you to end your spiritual growth at the top of the ladder—and there is no reason that you can't. Each of us has the unlimited potential to grow in Christ, but there's lots of hard work along the way.

The fourth Beatitude begins, *Blessed are those who hunger and thirst for righteousness. . . .* Even as you grow in Christ, you get discouraged at times. You just don't seem to have the power and victory that you need in your life. You are constantly hungering and thirsting for a consistent, righteous life.

God sent his Holy Spirit to earth on the Day of Pentecost to live within the hearts of men and women. The Holy Spirit has all the power you need in your life. God will give you a personal, unique language that can be a great tool in your life (Acts 2). The gifts of the Spirit will help you through every crisis (1 Corinthians 12). You will bear fruit of the Spirit daily (Galatians 5:22, 23). But these things happen only to those who are starving—who are hungering and thirsting—for this way of life. Hunger and thirst are the prerequisites for being filled more and more with the Holy Spirit of God. God's promise is sure: . . . *they will be filled.*

HUNGRY AND THIRSTY

Matt, an orphan, met Jesus when he was in high school, and the Lord so satisfied his need for a family that he decided to go on to Bible school to learn all he could about Jesus. He met his wife there, and they both anticipated being used in a special ministry someday. However, when they left the shelter of the Bible school, they found themselves lured by the world. They were both overworked in their zeal for material goods. As a result, they—and their children—were edgy. Tension filled their home.

An associate of Matt's came to him one day. This man actually knew less of the Bible, but he knew *more* about the nature of God—and he shared with Matt about the power that the Holy Spirit could give him. Matt's entire family developed a great desire for this power in their lives. They became so hungry they'd ask everyone they met, "Can you tell us about the Holy Spirit?"

One day Matt's wife met a woman who shared with her about the baptism of the Holy Spirit. That very evening, Matt invited the woman and her friends over to their home to pray and share about the Holy Spirit. The Holy Spirit so moved them that night that they wept and repented before God. The love they felt for Jesus filled their lives to such an extent that as they praised the Lord, they began to use words they had never learned. They had never known such joy!

That was a new beginning. Their family life was mended. They no longer felt a need to maintain their expensive wine collection. They threw a smashing "wine-pouring" party, literally, to pour their wine collection down the drain. They sold one of their cars to help alleviate their debts. They began a ministry in a nursing home where every week someone accepted the Lord. As much as they had ministered together in college, they had never seen that type of result from their ministry. They knew the Holy Spirit had made the difference, giving them a new vitality and courage. Their hunger and thirst was at last satisfied.

The next Beatitude says, *Blessed are the merciful . . . .* Being merciful means forgiving people who should know better for the evil things they do to you. Not those who *don't* know better, but those who *should* know better. Being merciful means that we don't hold resentment. We forgive our fellow-Christians even if we think they're making mistakes. Being merciful means seeing others as God sees them, whole and complete in Christ. It is only when we are filled with the Spirit of God that we can be truly merciful. And the Bible says that only when we are merciful to others do we reach the place where we stand blameless in the sight of God: *. . . they will be shown mercy.*

The next rung on the ladder is *Blessed are the pure in heart. . . .* The promise to those who are pure is that they will see God! Moses went up on Mount Sinai and saw God.

But God told him to cause the people to go away from the Mount; they were so impure that the brightness of God's appearing to Moses would kill them. When Moses came down from the Mount after seeing God, he descended in brightness. His face shone so brightly that the people could not look upon him. The Bible says that the pure in heart will live around the throne of God in heaven. They will be able to stand the brightness and glory of his presence because they are pure in heart.

How do we become pure in heart? It is a process that comes moment by moment, day by day, as we ask God to give us the mind of Christ. We must *choose* to think Christ's thoughts. We must discipline our lives to conform to his image. This is work. We need to ask God to help us think, speak, and act as Christ himself thought, spoke, and acted while he was on earth. As we grow into the likeness of Christ, we become purer in heart. And what a reward: *. . . they will see God.*

The seventh Beatitude is: *Blessed are the peacemakers . . .* There is no need for peacemakers unless there are wars. We are all involved in a war between God and Satan . . . between good and evil . . . between the health and salvation of God and the sickness and sin of the devil. To be a peacemaker, we need to enter the thick of the battle. We actually need to go into the war in order to win the peace.

If you are called upon to stop a fight between two persons, it means that you get in the middle, between the two. You risk getting hit from both sides! Often neither one of the warring parties ends up liking you for stopping the fight, but you have brought about a peace between them nevertheless. It's not always popular to be a peacemaker!

PEACEMAKER

John was a strong Christian leader and he led his business partner, Jay, to the Lord. He hadn't counted, however, on Jay becoming more successful in their commission-type business. John's jealousy kept him from helping Jay to grow in the Lord and read the Bible. Everyone could see

Jay's faults on the outside. No one could see John's faults on the inside, although both were equally in error before God. The break came when John decided to divide the business.

Needless to say, they couldn't agree on how to divide their holdings. They invited Bob, a mutual friend, to help them in this matter. Bob was mature in the Lord and he recognized his role as more than that of an adviser. He had been chosen by God to be a peacemaker. He was willing to give anything he had to bring about peace in both of these men's lives. He spent a great deal of his own money in helping them get to the root of their problem.

The business was dissolved. But more than that, John was healed of his jealousy and other resentments held since childhood. Jay began to read his Bible. Both men moved to new cities and are being used of God there. Bob, left behind, is no longer in communication with either man and has received no expression of appreciation for his advice. Like most peacemakers, he was rejected more than honored. His time and effort were unappreciated. He knows, however, that his reward lies far beyond what either man could say for or against him. No one has ever heard Bob say a word against either man. He has simply gone on to new ministries for the Lord.

Are you willing to enter the front lines of the battle and stand in the gap between warring sides? Are you willing to put yourself into a battle-scarring position? As you do—and fight and win battles and bring about peace for the Lord—the Bible promises that you shall be called a child of God. As his child, you become an heir of all God's blessings. You inherit his kingdom and all his heavenly riches: *. . . for they will be called sons of God.*

The next step on the ladder is: *Blessed are those who are persecuted because of righteousness. . . .* Are you willing to stand up for God in any situation, before any person, no matter the consequences? Now, many people are persecuted and all manner of evil is set against them, but it is not for righteousness' sake. It is not for God's sake. They may be persecuted as they stand up for fellowmen and good social causes, and they may be quite self-righteous about their stance, but this is not being

PROGRESSION IN THE BEATITUDES

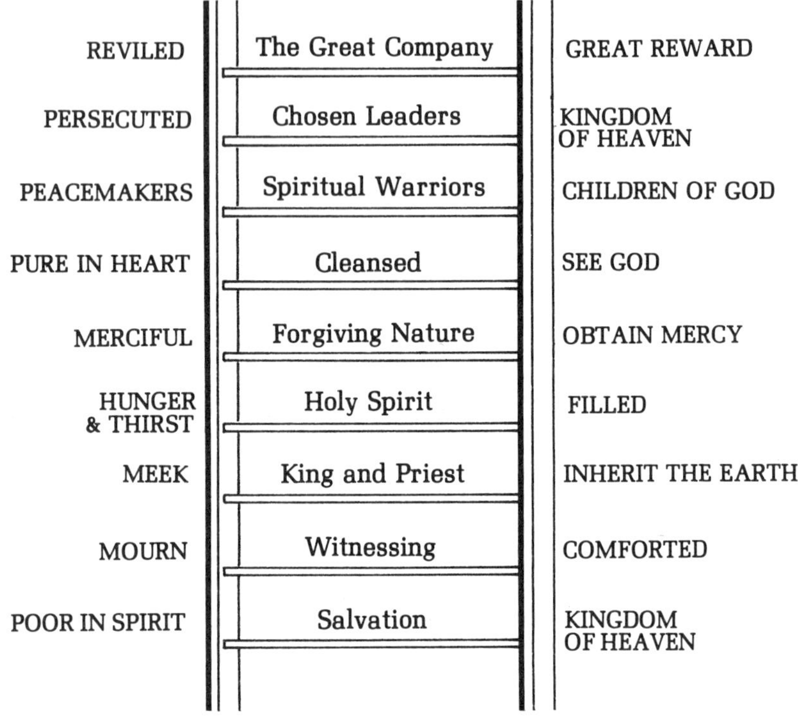

persecuted for righteousness' sake. It is only when we are truly willing to receive persecution—in words and deeds—for God's sake that we will attain the promised reward: . . . *for theirs is the kingdom of heaven.*

The final run on the ladder is closely related: *Blessed are you when people insult you, persecute you and falsely say all kinds of evil against you because of me.* . . . The Bible says that when you reach this place in your spiritual growth you can . . . *Rejoice and be glad, because great is your reward in heaven; for in the same way they persecuted the prophets who were before you.* You are in great company at the top of the ladder; the prophets of God are there with you!

Persecution didn't die in the third century. Thousands of Christians are undergoing severe persecution and even death in many countries of the world. Even in America, men and women are being reviled daily in the courts, press, and social clubs for their Christian stance.

In order to be persecuted, a person has to take such a bold stance for Christ that he or she offends the evil people around him. This passage is not talking just about being *willing* to be persecuted. It refers to actually living in such bold proclamation of Christ as all in all that evil men and women will revile you and persecute you and say all manner of evil things about you falsely. Jesus said, "No one has greater love than the one who lays down his life for his friends" (John 15:13). This is the same sacrifice that Jesus made. It is the supreme sacrifice. We no longer live for ourselves. We live totally for Christ. Everything we say and do is with the intent of lifting up Christ—no matter the consequences!

A great reward lies ahead for those who reach the top of the spiritual ladder described here in Matthew!

Did you find your place on the ladder? Do you sometimes feel as if you climb one step and then drop two? Ask God to help you grow—to fill you more and more with his Spirit so that you no longer waver as you grow into the image and likeness of Christ. Sometimes it is good for each of us to sit down and write a letter to God. Tell him what is on your mind. Tell him where you feel you are falling short, and ask his forgiveness. Ask him to help you grow with renewed strength. God wants to help you—he's just waiting for you to ask.

Do you see how a progression study works? The study we have just completed describes a progression in spiritual growth in the life of each Christian. Progressions lead us from one level of understanding to another. They are like stepping-stones on a path to a full understanding of who Christ is and what the kingdom of God is all about.

Science studies in school are often progressive. You have to learn one basic, simple fact before you can advance to another fact. One course becomes the basis for a more advanced course. Math studies are also that way. A student learns general math before progressing on to algebra, then geometry, and eventually trigonometry. One body of knowledge allows the student to have the proper background for entering another area of knowledge. Some chapters of the Bible are laid out in this same manner. One chapter flows into another chapter, which becomes the foundation for a third chapter.

The triune Psalms—22, 23, 24—form a good progression study as we seek an understanding of Jesus as a shepherd.

In Psalm 22 we see Jesus as the *Good* Shepherd who gives his life for his sheep. This is the crucified Christ.

In Psalm 23 we see Jesus as the *Great* Shepherd who is Owner of the flock. He lives with the flock and nurtures the flock. This is the resurrected Christ.

In Psalm 24 we see Jesus as the *Chief* Shepherd. He is the Shepherd of all shepherds—the supreme authority who reigns on earth.

I invite you now to turn to your Bible and to read the three chapters as a whole.

Now let's go back and look at each of the chapters in greater detail. Psalm 22 begins with the same words that Jesus spoke from the Cross: "My God, my God, why have you forsaken me?" (See Matthew 27:46.) We know at the very beginning of our study in this chapter that we are talking about the crucified Christ. The writings of David, the psalmist, have already been fulfilled. Jesus has already paid the price, giving up his life so that his sheep might live forever. This entire chapter is a great testimony that Christ is the Messiah!

Psalm 22:6-8 says:

But I am a worm and not a man, scorned by men and despised of the people. All who see me mock me; they hurl insults, shaking their heads: "He trusts in the Lord; let the Lord rescue him. Let him deliver him, since he delights in him."

When we read Matthew 27 we see that this is exactly what happened. As Jesus was crucified, he was taunted and reviled by men. Matthew 27:42, 43 says:

"He saved others," they said, "but he can't save himself! He's the king of Israel! Let him come down now from the cross, and we will believe in him. He trusts in God. Let God rescue him now if he wants him, for he said, 'I am the Son of God.' "

When David wrote his psalms—centuries before Jesus was born—he didn't know about crucifixion. He was a Jewish man, and the Jews didn't have crucifixions. Yet David described a Roman crucifixion without error. Psalm 22:14-18 says:

I am poured out like water, and all my bones are out of joint. My heart has turned to wax; it has melted away within me. My strength is dried up like a potsherd; and my tongue sticks to the roof of my mouth; you lay me in the dust of death. Dogs have surrounded me; a band of evil men has encircled me, they have pierced my hands and my feet. I can count all my bones; people stare and gloat over me. They divide my garments among them and cast lots for my clothing.

This is precisely what happened in the crucifixion of Christ. Death in crucifixion comes slowly. Hands and feet are nailed to a cross. The person hangs there until all the bones are pulled out of joint, and perspiration pours forth until there is no moisture in the body. The lungs eventually collapse and the heart bursts. The blood and perspiration mingle until the blood comes through the pores of the skin. John 19 describes how the soldiers cast lots for Jesus' garments, and how blood and water poured from Jesus when the soldiers pierced his side with a spear.

And then in Psalm 22:22 the mood shifts to praise!

I will declare your name to my brothers; in the congregation I will praise you.

And Psalm 22:26 adds:

The poor will eat and be satisfied; they who seek the Lord will praise him—may your hearts live forever!

Thus begins the glory of the resurrection! Up from the grave Jesus arose! Christ bore the Cross, gave up the ghost, and arose in total victory. Jesus purchased every part of our redemption. There is not one thing you've done or experienced that is beyond the price that Jesus paid. For this cause his name is to be praised! Those who seek the Lord Jesus Christ and praise him shall live forever!

This brings us then to Psalm 23. This is the psalm of provision. The price has been paid. Jesus is the Owner of the flock. He is the Shepherd and we are the sheep. It is important to note that the Shepherd and the sheep are of two different origins. Jesus is the only absolute authority. He is the Good Shepherd. He is of a different origin than we are. He is the Son of God, the crucified Lord. We, as human beings, cannot claim to have *his* absolute authority.

Psalm 23 begins:

The Lord is my shepherd, I shall lack nothing.

"Lack nothing" includes the fact that we aren't to worry about anything. The opposite of worry is saying, "I know who owns me and who is taking care of me."

The next verse says:

He makes me lie down in green pastures.

The green pastures represent our material provision. Jesus will provide whatever we need. He is *leading* us to that place of total provision where we can lie down to rest. Sheep don't march around a pasture to defend it. They relax, knowing that the shepherd protects them there. Jesus wants to lead us to a place in our spiritual lives where we can rest totally in him.

And then:

He leads me beside quiet waters.

This refers to the Holy Spirit of God and the gifts of the Spirit. See 1 Corinthians 12, 13, 14. The Holy Spirit is referred to in Scripture as a river of living water. We dwell as Jesus' sheep in a green pasture, and we drink from the living water of the Holy Spirit!

Psalm 23:3 says:

He restores my soul.

Your soul is your personality—your desires, your values, your choices. Have you ever felt totally depleted? You've given until you think you don't have anything left to give? You need restoration. You need someone to encourage you, to build you up, to compliment you. There is only one person who can restore your soul. It isn't your husband or wife or your minister or best friend. It is Jesus. Only he can restore your identity and fill the areas of void in your life.

He guides me in paths of righteousness for his name's sake.

Jesus promises to lead us, to give us direction and the discipline we need to live a righteous life. In the process we take his name. We become *Christ*-ians. We live in his name and for his cause.

Even though I walk through the valley of the shadow of death, I will fear no evil, for you are with me; your rod and your staff, they comfort me.

Are you really convinced in your spirit that God will take care of you? He promises you that. You do not need to live in fear of the world events or the evil that fills our newspapers—murders, rapes, tornadoes, earthquakes, or terrorists' bombs. The Bible says that the Lord gives us a spirit of love and peace and of a sound mind—*not* a spirit of fear. Fear comes from Satan.

How do we overcome fear? By believing that the rod and staff of Jesus protect us! A shepherd's rod is a short, straight stick that has a ball at one end. It is used to gently nudge the sheep's feet. The rod refers to correction.

God will correct us if we are about to make an error that would get us off his path and result in harm to us. The staff is our defense system in Christ. A shepherd's staff is a long stick with a crook at one end. It's used to snatch the enemy by the jugular vein! Let the Good Shepherd take care of the wolves! Trust in God's promises to protect and deliver you.

You prepare a table before me in the presence of my enemies. You anoint my head with oil; my cup overflows.

God promises you a personal table of material and spiritual food that will meet your needs. Even if you are surrounded on all sides by enemies—or by famine, drought, or lack of spiritual food—he will take care of you. You are his chosen child. The anointing with oil is your inauguration as a king and priest—a ruler in God's spiritual kingdom. When you fully grasp this fact—that God loves you, protects you, and establishes you as a ruler of a kingdom that will last forever—you will not be able to contain the joy. It will spill over and bless every area of your life! You will be able to proclaim with the psalmist:

Surely goodness and love will follow me all the days of my life, and I will dwell in the house of the Lord forever.

And now, are you ready for the capstone? Psalm 24 proclaims Jesus as the Shepherd of shepherds, the Lord of lords! Everything on earth ultimately belongs to him.

Psalm 24:1 begins:

The earth is the Lord's, and everything in it, the world, and all who live in it.

The whole earth belongs to God! When you grasp that fact, you can have no doubt that God is able to supply all your needs. If God calls you to a task, he has the finances and the means to help you complete the task. All the earth belongs to him! He is in charge of every natural law. He has all energy resources at his fingertips. He created the world—"founded it upon the seas and established it upon the floods"—and the Creator knows the creation.

First Peter 5:4 promises that we will have a part in claiming the earth as our own:

And when the Chief Shepherd appears, you will receive the crown of glory that will never fade away.

How do we qualify for this crown? The psalmist asked the same question:

Who may ascend the hill of the Lord? Who may stand in his holy place?

The answer follows. The person who does these four things:

He who has clean hands . . . the one who does right,
and a pure heart . . . the one who thinks right,
who does not lift up his soul to an idol . . . who is totally devoted to God and others,
or sworn by what is false . . . the one who speaks right.

Think, speak, and act without selfishness and you shall

. . . receive blessing from the Lord and vindication from God.

What a great privilege! We are called to be joint heirs with the King of Glory—the Lord, mighty and strong in battle. The promise of everlasting life is ours.

Do you see how our understanding about Jesus flows from chapter to chapter in these Psalms?

In Psalm 22, Jesus is the Good Shepherd, the crucified Lord. In him is our salvation.

In Psalm 23, Jesus is the Caretaker of the Church. He is the Leader of all Christians, the Great Shepherd who keeps his flock.

In Psalm 24, Jesus is the Chief Shepherd who has all

PROGRESSION IN THE TRIUNE PSALMS

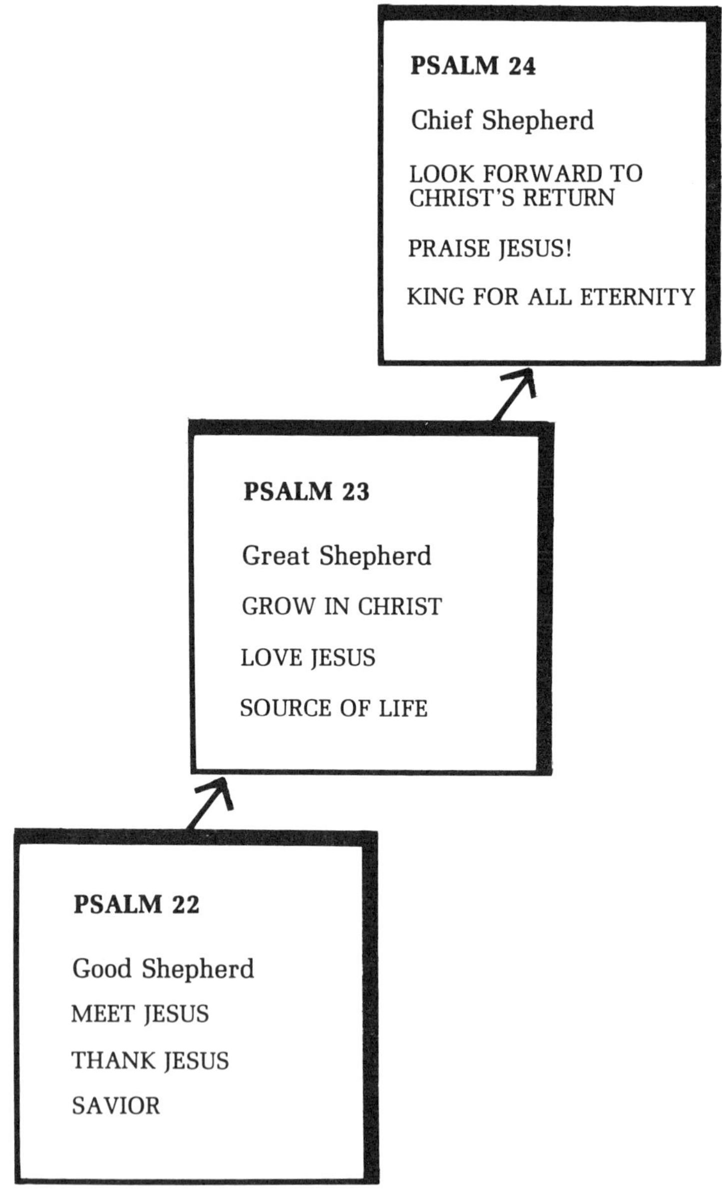

power in heaven and earth. In him is our hope of eternal life. In him is our inheritance of the earth and a home in heaven's glory.

Or stated another way:

We meet Jesus at the Cross (Psalm 22).
We grow in Christ in our daily lives (Psalm 23).
We look forward to Christ's return and the establishment of his kingdom (Psalm 24).

Or . . .

We thank Jesus for loving us enough to die for us (Psalm 22).
We love Jesus and honor his will in our lives (Psalm 23).
We praise Jesus as King of kings (Psalm 24).

Now . . .

We see Jesus as our Savior *at the Cross* (Psalm 22).
He is our Source *of life as we walk with him* (Psalm 23).
He is our King *for all eternity as we anticipate his return* (Psalm 24).

Our understanding *progresses* as we move from the Cross to the crown and as we grow in our relationship with Christ.

These are only two progression studies. The Bible has many others. As you read the Bible, stop to ask yourself occasionally, "Are these Scriptures related in a progressive way?" This may happen especially as you are reading strings of words or Scriptures that seem to be a list of truths. Here are a few suggestions for some progression studies you may want to do on your own:

To begin with, take a second look at Psalm 23. This is really a progression within a progression. Note how a Christian moves from accepting the Lord as Shepherd . . . to seeing the Lord as Provider in every area of life . . . to regarding the Lord as Protector in all circumstances . . . to accepting a royal appointment in God's kingdom . . . to anticipating the eternal dwelling-place the believer has in heaven!

Galatians 5:22, 23 provides a good progression study. Note how one characteristic gives rise to the next as we bear the fruit of the Spirit.

Ephesians 3:14-19 is a spiritual progression for those who pray with boldness and confidence in their access to God. This refers to those with a strong prayer-life. Look for a progression in what God will give to the one who prays.

First Thessalonians 5:16-18 is a progression for those who are living in the day of the Lord's return—us! The progression tells us how believers are to unite together to form a strong network in the last days.

And now, remember these key guidelines as you engage in a progression study:

Read the whole before you dissect the part.
Look for a strong relationship among the verses. Be wary of contriving a relationship that doesn't exist.
Check your progression with other Scriptures. Is your interpretation of the passage supported by other passages in the Bible? If not, you're on the wrong track.
The last verse or last passage must bring you closer to Jesus than the first.

Realize that progressions always lead upward! They always point to growth in our understanding or relationship with Jesus.

These studies will encourage you to seek new heights in your relationship with God. I encourage your quest!

TYPE AND SHADOW STUDIES

Have you ever stopped to really look at shadows? Most of us are familiar with our own shadow. We grow up knowing that our shadow follows us and that we can make images of animals on tent and cabin walls while at slumber parties or on camping trips.

Look around you. See the variety of shadows. Some may be cast by lamps or lighting fixtures. Others may be cast by the sun, candles, or moonlight.

Note two characteristics about shadows. First, shadows mirror objects. Shadows are *not* objects, but they have the same overall shape as the objects that are between the light source and the shadow.

Second, shadows are not even in their degree of darkness. Shadows do not have details, but they do have different intensities of darkness. The brighter the light and the closer the object to the light, the more distinct the shadow.

The Bible has interesting things to say about shadows. Colossians 2:17 refers to "things which are a mere shadow of what is to come; but the substance belongs to Christ." Hebrews 8:4, 5 refers to another aspect of shadows: ". . . since there are those who offer the gifts

*Scripture references in this chapter are from the *New American Standard Version.*

according to the Law; who serve a copy and shadow of the heavenly things . . ." Here we are told that the people and incidents of the Old Testament are objects that have spiritual shadows.

One of the most rewarding ways of studying the Old Testament is to look for the people, objects, and events that cast spiritual shadows. These studies reflect "types" of experiences and events that happen to us on a spiritual level today. In themselves, the stories are about Old Testament people and events. They may be journeys—and may be studied as journeys. They are historical happenings.

The *shadows* of these stories tell us more about God, outlining for us the nature and working of God on the spiritual level. They also tell us more about our spiritual selves. They deal with our inner person—the "real" person inside us who will live forever.

As we enter type and shadow studies, we see plays or dramas within the Scriptures. Let's take as an example the story of Ruth, Naomi, and Boaz.

THE BOOK OF RUTH

Dramatis Personae

Naomi . . . . *The Holy Spirit*
Ruth. . . . . *You*
Boaz . . . . *Jesus*

Servants . . . . *Ministers of the Word*
Maids . . . . *Strong believers*
Grainfields . . . . *Word of God*

Native land. . . . . *Your carnal nature*
Bethlehem. . . . . *The spiritual place where God's plan for you on earth is fulfilled; Jesus' birthplace*

I encourage you to stop at this point to read the four chapters of the Book of Ruth.

ACT 1

In the first act of this story, Ruth and her sister-in-law, Orpah, are both widowed. Their mother-in-law, Naomi, comes to them and tells them that she is returning to her homeland. Ruth and her sister-in-law were very close. They had shared a common heartache. Now they are both called upon to make a choice: to go with Naomi or to return to their parents' homes.

The Holy Spirit will come to you also with this question: "Will you follow me or will you return to your sinful life?" The Holy Spirit may speak to your best friend or your spouse in the same manner. You and your best friend may not make the same decision. Ruth and Orpah didn't. Ruth chose to follow the wooing of the Holy Spirit. Orpah returned home.

We stand or fall before God as individuals. Each of us must make our own decision when the Holy Spirit approaches us. We are not judged by our parents', husband's, or wife's decision. Each of us is responsible for our own spiritual growth.

Ruth said:

"Do not urge me to leave you or turn back from following you; for where you go, I will go, and where you lodge, I will lodge. Your people shall be my people, and your God, my God. Where you die, I will die, and there I will be buried. Thus may the Lord do to me, and worse, if anything but death parts you and me" (Ruth 1:16, 17).

What a commitment to the Holy Spirit—to go wherever the Holy Spirit leads, to accept all Christians as "my people," to even die for Christ! Few of us are able to respond to the wooing of the Holy Spirit with such commitment. Most of us make this commitment in bits and pieces all the way through life. It takes awhile before we are ready to fully accept *all* Christians as our brothers and sisters. It's easier for some of us to accept only the lovely and talented Christians—those with whom we agree—as our relatives in the Lord. For others, it's easier to befriend only those we see as beneath us—*less* lovely or less talented. It takes some of us awhile before we will say, "I'll follow you, Holy Spirit, no matter whom I encounter or how tough the circumstances." We'd prefer our life in Christ to be easy—to always feel acceptance, love, peace, and joy.

Ruth *attached* herself to the Holy Spirit wholeheartedly. She broke away from her old life completely. The Bible says in Ruth 1:18 that Ruth was *"determined"* to go.

ACT 2

Ruth 1:19 tells us that Ruth and Naomi then made a trip. They journeyed to Bethlehem, the birthplace of God on earth. You will also make a journey with the Holy Spirit through a spiritual desert. No enemies will come after you. You will face no temptations. But you will feel dry and separated from others. The Bible tells us that there is a great separation between the godly and ungodly—a great gulf between the righteous and the unrighteous. As you follow the Holy Spirit, you will become more and more detached from your old habits and your old way of life. This will be a lonely journey—just you and the Holy Spirit.

ACT 3

The second chapter of Ruth begins by telling us that "Naomi had a kinsman of her husband, a man of great wealth, of the family of Elimelech, whose name was Boaz" (Ruth 2:1).

The Holy Spirit has a kinsman also: Jesus.

Ruth asked Naomi for permission to work for Boaz. She said, "Please let me go to the field and glean among the ears of grain after one in whose sight I may find favor." And she said to her, "Go, my daughter" (Ruth 2:2).

When you meet Jesus fully—face-to-face—you will love everything about him. You will love all that he possesses and does, and you will want to know everything about him. The Bible tells us that the Word of God is bread—or food—for our souls. These grainfields of Boaz are a shadow of the spiritual fields we find in the pages of the Bible.

In your hunger to know more about Jesus and to live a life patterned after his, you will turn to the Bible. You will want to plow through the pages of the Bible—gleaning the truths that are on every page. The Bible will be a field for you and you will want to glean in that field daily, as in subject studies. You will not be content to have others reap for you. As Ruth, you will want to follow after the reapers and gather biblical truths for yourself.

We also find a warning here. Boaz says to Ruth,

> *"Listen carefully, my daughter. Do not go to glean in another field; furthermore, do not go on from this one, but stay here with my maids. Let your eyes be on the field which they reap, and go after them"* (Ruth 2:8).

As you glean truths from the Bible, you will become excited about spiritual experiences and the spiritual growth in your life. You may have a tendency to seek out other spiritual experiences or wonder if more truth is available in other religions. Our world is filled with literature about various metaphysical experiences. Jesus cautions us immediately: stay out of those fields, stay in the Bible, stay in Christian fellowship. Attend church and Bible studies. Work with the other believers or "maids" in Boaz's field. Let the servants of God take care of you and nurture you.

Do you know how cults and false religions arise? Cult leaders invariably emphasize only one particle or a few particles of truth. Truth is as the sands of the sea. Some people look at the beach and see a particular grain of sand glistening in the sunlight. They say to themselves, "This grain of sand—this grain of truth—glistens more than all the rest." And they pick up that grain of truth out of the surrounding truths, build a platform for it, and in the process cover up the rest of the truth. Entire organizations have been built this way.

Jesus warns us about this and tells us not to look at the other fields. Boaz said to Ruth, "Let your eyes be on the field which they reap. . . ." Temptation always begins with what we see or what we imagine in our "mind's eye." Eve "saw that the tree was good" (Genesis 3:6).

Then in Ruth 2:9 Boaz says:

"Indeed, I have commanded the servants not to touch you. When you are thirsty, go to the water jars and drink from what the servants draw."

Boaz tells Ruth to let the servants draw the water for her. As a new Christian, you are not able to draw upon your own power. You will need to drink of the power of the Holy Spirit. The water in this passage is a shadow of the baptism of the Holy Spirit that was poured out upon all believers in the New Testament. This water is there—already drawn by the servants of God—for you to drink when you are spiritually thirsty! The baptism of the Holy Spirit is available—ready and waiting—for you, too, when you want it.

ACT 4

Boaz says to Ruth in 2:11, 12:

"All that you have done for your mother-in-law after the death of your husband has been fully reported to me, and how you left your father and your mother and the land of your birth, and came to a people that you did not previously know. May the Lord reward your work, and your wages be full from the Lord, the God of Israel, under whose wings you have come to seek refuge."

Jesus says this to us:

"I know all about you. I know how you made the decision to leave your carnal nature. I see how you have crossed a spiritual wilderness and have given up your worldly associations for my sake. I see how you glean only in my fields. I see that when you were thirsty, you came to drink of the waters that were drawn for you from my

wells. I know all about your sufferings and your loneliness. And I will see that you are rewarded."

Jesus lives today as our Intercessor at the throne of God. He communicates to God directly for us—that our sins might be forgiven and that we might receive a full inheritance, an abundant life, from God. He sees us, knows us completely, loves us thoroughly, and is our Advocate before God.

Ruth 2:14 says that

. . . at mealtime Boaz said to her, "Come here, that you may eat of the bread and dip your piece of bread in the vinegar." So she sat beside the reapers; and he served her roasted grain, and she ate and was satisfied and had some left.

The time comes when Jesus sits with you and teaches you personally how to feed your soul from the Word. He will give you the full strength of the Bible—the mature "parched corn" of the Bible's truth (even your own progression and type and shadow studies to chew on). This food will meet your deep spiritual needs.

Ruth was given the full riches of the field—the food from Boaz's hands and the best gleaning position in the field. Some truth is given to us by direct revelation from God through intensive study. Other truth we glean in fellowship with others who are studying God's Word.

At the end of each day, Ruth went home to Naomi. We, too, must check our gleanings in the presence of the Holy Spirit. We must subject our truth to inspection. We must allow the Holy Spirit to confirm the lessons we think we have learned in the Bible.

See Ruth 2:15, 16:

When she rose to glean, Boaz commanded his servants, saying, "Let her glean even among the sheaves, and do not insult her. And also you shall purposely pull out for her some grain from the bundles and leave it that she may glean, and do not rebuke her."

Ruth "rose to glean." The time will come when you, too, need to leave the spiritual table with Jesus and get out into daily life. Jesus has bundles of blessing awaiting you in everyday experiences. Because you have eaten at his table, he purposely has special blessings pulled out just for you, to make your day easier. Pick them up. Don't stumble over these blessings. Be aware. Anticipate these daily love gifts from the Lord and appreciate them in your life.

ACT 5

Ruth stayed in Boaz's field through two harvests. Ruth 2:23 says:

So she stayed close by the maids of Boaz in order to glean until the end of the barley harvest and the wheat harvest. And she lived with her mother-in-law.

Ruth's commitment was a *continuing* commitment. She didn't glean awhile and then quit. By staying for the second harvest Ruth was able to help new gleaners—or new believers—to understand the Word. This was a commitment of both time and energy.

Ruth also had to make a commitment to follow the leading of the Holy Spirit, even if it meant doing something "out of the ordinary." Ruth 3:4, 5 says:

"And it shall be when he lies down, that you shall notice the place where he lies, and you shall go and uncover his feet and lie down; then he will tell you what you shall do." And she said to her, "All that you say I will do."

This was not an ordinary thing for Ruth to do. It was an unlikely action. She was taking a great risk. Boaz owned the field; Ruth was only a gleaner. It was very bold for her to enter his presence uninvited. Nevertheless, she *obeyed.* She knew that the Holy Spirit was speaking to her, and she did as she was told.

A similar incident happened in the New Testament

when Mary anointed the feet of Jesus with costly perfume (John 12:1-8 or Luke 7:36-50). She was ridiculed for wasting her expensive possession; yet she *knew* she was to bathe Jesus' feet with her perfume. She was rewarded by the praise of Jesus himself for her obedience. When the Holy Spirit prompts *you* to do something, you must obey—even if it seems contrary to normal expectations.

ACT 6

Naomi advised Ruth in 3:18—

"Wait, my daughter, until you know how the matter turns out; for the man will not rest until he has settled it today."

Jesus also tells us to wait, to sit still awhile. That is the position in which we find ourselves today. Jesus has returned to heaven. He has given us a measure of grain: the promises in his Word that he will come again for us and claim us as his bride. Just as Boaz went into the city to redeem Ruth as his bride, so Jesus has gone to purchase our full redemption, to prepare a heavenly home for us, and to fight the battles and pay the costs that will make it possible for us to inherit the earth with him. We must wait expectantly. We must be ready for his return.

Boaz did return for Ruth! Ruth 4:9 says:

Then Boaz said to the elders and all the people, "You are witnesses today that I have bought from the hand of Naomi all that belonged to Elimelech and all that belonged to Chilion and Mahlon. Moreover, I have acquired Ruth the Moabitess, the widow of Mahlon, to be my wife in order to raise up the name of the deceased on his inheritance, so that the name of the deceased may not be cut off from his brothers or from the court of his birthplace; you are witnesses today."

Just as surely, Jesus will return for us! He will come saying, "I have purchased this earth. My bride, who is a widow of a former life, will have a *new* name and a *new* inheritance."

ACT 7

When Jesus returns for us, he will establish us as rulers of this earth. The entire world will know that we are the bride of Christ, just as Boaz let the entire city know that Ruth was his bride.

Do you know the reason Boaz took Ruth as his wife? It was not only as a reward for her faithfulness and devotion. Ruth 4:13 says:

So Boaz took Ruth, and she became his wife, and he went in to her. And the Lord enabled her to conceive, and she gave birth to a son.

That son was the grandfather of David. And from the line of David, Jesus was born. Jesus was born in the city of Boaz and Ruth: Bethlehem.

Ruth 4:16 says:

Then Naomi took the child and laid him in her lap, and became his nurse.

Those whom you lead to the Lord will also be nurtured by the Holy Spirit.

Do you see what a great and wonderful plan God had for Ruth all along? He has that same plan for us. When Jesus returns for us and establishes us as his bride here on earth, the final redemption of the world will rest in our hands. We will be the helpmate of Jesus—co-inheritors of his glory and co-workers in the harvest fields!

Notice as you study Ruth that a great progression study arises *within* the type and shadow study. This is found in Ruth 3:3:

"Wash yourself therefore, and anoint yourself and put on your best clothes, and go down to the threshing floor;

but do not make yourself known to the man until he has finished eating and drinking."

These are specific instructions from the Holy Spirit to us:

1. Wash yourself therefore . . . *receive the thorough cleansing of your sins and hang-ups by the blood of Jesus. Get rid of the fear and psychological excuses you've kept in your life. Allow them to be washed away.*
2. Anoint yourself . . . *with the baptism of the Holy Spirit. You must choose to receive this blessing.*
3. Put on your best clothes . . . *or your robe of righteousness. You weave this robe yourself by "right living" and by making Christlike choices daily.*
4. Go down to the threshing floor . . . *even though you are dressed in your best, as if to parade the streets of the city. You are to go to a place where you are willing to sacrifice all for God in the lowliest place of service on earth. Be able to take the insults of a lowly position without allowing them to hurt. Be ready to lay down your life for Christ in the least likely of places.*
5. Do not make yourself known to the man . . . *Don't point out your accomplishments to Jesus or to anyone else with pride. Jesus knows what you're doing and where to find you when the time comes for him to reward you. In the meantime, keep a low profile.*

This is a study within a study!

Ruth is a type and shadow of what has come to pass and also what *will* come to pass. As we live out the story of Ruth in our lives today, we move to a deeper walk with Jesus.

Another type and shadow study is found in Deuteronomy. This is the story of the children of Israel and the course they followed to the promised land.

This is a good place to recall the difference between a journey study and a type and shadow study. A journey study gives us direction for our *natural lives.* It helps us to understand how we should feel in circumstances and what we should do in situations on a day-to-day basis. A type and shadow study, on the other hand, helps us to understand our *spiritual purpose*—not only as we have lived and are living it here on earth, but also how we will live it in the future and throughout all eternity. Journey studies show us God's working in our natural lives—that God is with us and will reward our faithfulness to him. Type and shadow studies show us the master plan for our lives in the context of eternity!

A type and shadow study also differs from a progression study as we saw in the examination of Ruth 3:3. In a progression study we are aware of the *steps* that occur in spiritual growth. A type and shadow study tells us *how* these steps occur and why. They reveal the interplay of the Holy Spirit and Jesus in our lives as we make the steps.

The story of the Israelites in Deuteronomy shows that spiritual interplay in a clear and beautiful way.

The Book of Deuteronomy is the writing of Moses to the children of Israel just before the children were to inherit the promised land—just before they crossed over the Jordan River and entered the special piece of real estate that God had prepared for them.

Today, we also stand on the brink of the Jordan River—just on the brink of inheriting the fullness of God's promises to us. This will be the special state where we live in *all* the promises of God. The words of Moses echo down through the ages to us as a direct type and shadow of our exodus from sin to the point of living in the "promised land" of God.

Deuteronomy 2:24 says:

> *"Arise, set out, and pass through the valley of Arnon. Look! I have given Sihon the Amorite, king of Heshbon, and his land into your hand; begin to take possession and contend with him in battle. This day I will begin to put the dread and fear of you upon the peoples everywhere under the heavens, who, when they hear the report of you, shall tremble and be in anguish because of you."*

This is God's command to us today. He says, "It's time to act. You know my commandments. You have wandered daily under my guidance. Now is the time for the promises to come to fruition. Rise up and take action!"

Now this valley was not the valley of the Jordan River. It was not the last step before the children inherited the promised land. The Ar River at the edge of this valley was a boundary line between two countries. It was a deep and muddy river. It was an obstacle in the path. God wasn't going to part these waters for the children. They had to cross the river on their own.

Perhaps you have an obstacle in your life today. Perhaps you are facing a muddy, troubled situation and you're camped on the banks of the Ar River—just sitting, waiting for something to happen. Perhaps you think God will act supernaturally to divide the waters as he did at the Red Sea, or that the river will dry up, or that you will sprout wings to fly across. Not so. (God parted the Red Sea for your escape from Egypt—which is a type and shadow of your bondage to sin and the world. That escape *always* requires supernatural intervention by God.)

The Ar River in your life may be doubt. It may be fear. It may be a personal habit. It may be a situation in your marriage, family life, social life, or church life. Some obstacle may be keeping you from moving on.

Many women face an obstacle of fear of spiritual growth. They are afraid they will be stronger in the Lord than their husbands. They are camped on the river banks, waiting for their husbands to cross first. They say to God, "I don't want to get closer to you than my husband is." I don't see any place in the Bible where the God of the universe accepts that excuse from anyone.

Perhaps you are afraid that your neighbors and friends will ostracize you if you get closer to God. Perhaps you are afraid that you will lose touch with your children. Perhaps you are afraid that if you obey God you will have to give up many of your social pleasures (not realizing that the friendships you will make with believers will be so much more meaningful and will last forever).

God calls you to cross the river. You are an individual

standing alone before God. You and you alone are responsible to him for your soul.

God says that when you are bold enough to wade into the river—knowing full well that you will get messy and wet in the process—that God will put dread and fear into your enemies so they will let you pass safely through the valley.

Can you accept that from God today? *You* won't scare the enemies of your soul into letting you alone. *God* puts that fear and dread into their hearts.

Israel crossed over the Ar River and proceeded to pass through the Arnon Valley. Moses sent messengers to the king of the land to say:

> *"Let me pass through your land. I will travel only on the highway; I will not turn aside to the right or to the left. You will sell me food for money so that I may eat, and give me water for money so that I may drink, only let me pass through on foot . . . until I cross over the Jordan into the land which the Lord our God is giving to us"* (Deuteronomy 2:27-29).

This was the land of the Amorites, a people who were not really the staunch enemies of the children of Israel as much as they were people who *also* considered themselves chosen of God. They were the descendants of Lot. They were self-righteous people, "do-gooders." In many ways, these are the *greatest* enemies to Christians. "Good" is always the enemy of "best!"

The children of Israel said to the Amorites, "We want to do you no harm. We simply want to pass through this area, paying and working as we go. We don't want your land; we just want to move on through to our land."

But the Amorite king didn't see things their way. The children of God moved ahead anyway. And the Bible says that when the dust from the battles settled, the children of Israel had destroyed the people of the land completely and decisively. They left no survivors.

The entire area of "good works" will someday belong to Christians. God is saying through this shadow that the entire activity of helping others—the sick, those in need, those in prison—will fall to Christians. The "do-gooders" will not be able to accept Christian principles in their midst; they will not give the glory to God or admit that God is the source of their strength and ability to do good. As a result, God will give these areas of responsibility to his chosen people.

We are not to become like the Amorites. We are not to follow the systems, codes, or little tidbits of self-righteousness that they represented. We are *not* to rely upon ourselves to set up good works or to do good for others. The area of good works is not our final destination. The Israelites captured all the cities in the valley and destroyed all the people, and they moved on. We are to do the same—taking over charitable work, giving honor to God as we march on toward our goal. For example, we are to visit and care for those in nursing homes and hospitals—but we are to go beyond. We are *also* to pray for them and tell them about Jesus and his love for them and his power to set them free!

God gave the children the material systems of that valley—the goods, social structures, and wealth—in order that the children might have the means to walk on to inherit the true promised land. God will also give his children in this day the material means to further God's kingdom and to reach the promised land. We are not to get bogged down in the social systems. We are to move past them, through them, and beyond to a fuller existence in God.

When the children of Israel arrived in the hill country (Pisgah) to the east of the Jordan River, they conquered the land there and established homes and a city (Deuteronomy 3:18-29). The children of Israel were told to establish a post in this place and to send out their warriors from this fortress.

Do you know whom the children had to conquer in order to set up their community on the banks of the Jordan? Og. Og and his descendants were the last of the giants. Og is a type and shadow of Satan and his demons. After the children conquered the Amorites (the "do-gooders"), they were forced into the battle with the giants themselves. These enemies were of a different breed—hostile, out for blood, aggressive . . . and big! Just read about the dimensions of Og's bed in Deuteronomy 3:11! In modern-day measurements, that bed was six feet wide and thirteen and a half feet long!

Deuteronomy 3:2 says:

"But the Lord said to me, 'Do not fear him, for I have delivered him and all his people and his land into your hand; and you shall do to him just as you did to Sihon king of the Amorites, who lived at Heshbon.' "

We do not have to fear Satan. Do you fully realize that? God has called you to do battle with Satan, and he has already won that battle even before he calls you into it. He has given you the power and authority to crush Satan, just as the children of Israel crushed Og. The passage says that the cities in Og were surrounded by high walls and fortified with heavy iron gates and bars, but the children of God destroyed everyone and took the livestock and the spoils of the area for their own. Satan's systems seem strong—the cities walled, fortified with gates and bars—but the children of God today will overcome even the most secure stronghold.

The Amorites couldn't defeat Og. But the children of Israel could—and *did!*

When the children reached the banks of the Jordan, they were not to forge "full steam ahead" across the river. They were told to stop, regroup their forces, claim the land, establish a community among themselves, and strengthen those warriors who were to venture first to capture the promised land.

God is calling his children today to be closely committed to one another in loyalty and caring. This commitment will be a launching pad for entering and possessing the promised land. The children of Israel needed the city on the banks of the Jordan. They needed the material wealth there in order to outfit their armies. God had promised them a land, and now he equipped them to fight for that promise.

We are in that position today. God has us on the banks of the Jordan—just opposite the promised land. He has given us a place to occupy. We are to take the material possessions that once belonged to Og and to fortify ourselves for the battles ahead. We are to have a strong sense of caring for one another. We are to unite and work together as Christians on the eve of our entry into the fullness of God's promises.

It is important to note that twelve tribes were united in that task—not just one large tribe. Today believers represent many cultures, countries, and denominations. We are not being called to melt ourselves together into one organization. We are to be united, however, in our *commitment* to the Lord Jesus Christ and to the task ahead.

We must know the Word of God. We must have fellowship with believers. We must be ready at a moment's notice—fully equipped and personally fit—to enter the promised land. And we are to wait and watch for God's command to action.

Today we are on the edge of the banks of the river—waiting for the signal to cross. We are not living in the promised land yet! We see miracles of God in our lives every day and hear about them through testimonies of others. We see glimpses of a coming glory—although no one today is *fully* living in *all* the promises—when we will be able to cast mountains into the sea, heal the sick as our shadows fall upon them, or multiply the loaves to feed the multitudes. That day is coming! What an exciting prospect as we gaze across the river with Joshua to the "fair land" and "good hill country" beyond (Deuteronomy 3:25)! How wonderful to anticipate *living in all the promises of God to us in the Bible—every day!*

Many other passages of the Bible may also be studied as types and shadows.

Here are four suggestions for studies to do on your own. Each one is a book of the Old Testament:

Esther
Jonah
Job
Joshua

As you read a book, see how this book fits into the overall pattern of the Bible. Note where it has been placed in the Bible and how it relates to other books. Begin to see the master plan for the entire Bible. (Note: The Bible is *not* arranged in chronological order.) Begin to see the Bible as a whole, with one central theme and purpose.

Again, these are studies that spill over into one another. The truth of one study confirms the truth of another. Precepts are built upon precepts. Lines are built upon lines. Passages are built upon passages. Relationships are to be drawn slowly and carefully over the months as one passage illuminates another passage.

These are studies that show us how truth is acquired—each grain of sand contributing to the entire beach of truth.

SYMBOL STUDIES

You may ask, "What are the symbols in the Bible?"

There are many. Numbers are symbols. Colors are used as symbols. Tangible objects can be symbols.

Symbols have been used by God to bring the meaning of the entire Bible into clear perspective. They occur in every book of the Bible. In many instances, understanding a symbol is the key to understanding an entire story or teaching. Symbols indicate *eternal* value, eternal meaning, and eternal reasons.

As awesome and important as symbols are in the Bible, they are among the easiest signposts of truth to spot and interpret—especially the *objects* identified with the Jewish people.

I'd like to take as an example of a symbol the Ark of the Covenant, the most important object in the worship of the Israelites.

Before we begin, I encourage you to read Exodus 37. This chapter gives the specific details about the construction of the Ark.

The premise for our symbol study is this:

THE ARK OF THE COVENANT	=	DEVOUT BELIEVERS IN THIS LAST GENERATION

*Scripture references in this chapter are from the *King James Version*.

The Ark of the Covenant was located in the holiest part of the Tabernacle, where the Israelites came to worship and to make their sacrifices. The Ark was a piece of furniture, a vessel, which contained certain items. It was a symbol to the people of God's presence with them. To the Israelites, the Ark was the very dwelling-place of the glory of Almighty God! To all other peoples, the Ark was a symbol of the Israelites' strength.

We are the symbol of God's strength and presence on this earth today. Other people cannot see God; they cannot even see Jesus. But they do see us. Paul said to the Corinthians, "Ye are our epistle written in our hearts, known and read of all men . . . written not with ink, but with the Spirit of the Living God; not in tables of stone, but in fleshy tables of the heart" (2 Corinthians 3:2, 3). He also said, "We have this treasure in earthen vessels, that the excellency of the power may be of God, and not of us" (See 2 Corinthians 4:7).

Others watch our lives to see if we are the vessels of the Spirit of Almighty God. We *are* the Ark of the Covenant in our world—the testimony of what God is doing, where he dwells on earth, and how he works in the twentieth century. We are the living presence of God to all people dwelling on earth that they might observe that God is at work. We are a recognizable symbol to unbelievers that God is keeping his covenant with man.

The Ark is also called the Ark of Testimony or the Ark of Witness. God calls us to witness to his good news, Jesus. The Ark is called in yet another place a "holy Ark." The Lord calls us to holiness, too. First Peter 1:16 says, "Be ye holy; for I am holy."

GOD'S COVENANT OR PROMISES FOR US TODAY

No images or statues of God were placed in the Ark (Exodus 20:4). God dwelt in the Ark with his invisible presence—the shekinah glory. Today he is counting on us to bear his name and to witness to his power in like manner. He is an invisible presence that fills our lives.

As God's living symbols of his presence and promise, we

must bear the same characteristics and functions as the Ark in the Old Testament. What was true for the Ark must hold true for us in a symbolic sense.

The Ark was built after the Israelites had been out of Egypt's bondage for a little more than a year. It was not built overnight; it was built carefully and slowly, according to a precise master plan. In the same way, our lives are restructured by God after we leave the bondage of sin. A holy life doesn't happen suddenly. Just as surely, God has a plan—*a precise plan and reason*—for bringing us into his perfection.

THE ARK

WOOD = HUMAN NATURE

Let's take a look at the Ark itself, its form and substance.

We read that the Ark was made basically of acacia wood, an earthly substance. Wood grows out of the dust of the earth. We as human beings have that same characteristic. We are creatures of this earth. We aren't angels! We are human, fallible flesh. God knows the materials that he uses in his creation, and we must accept who we are: *human beings*.

GOLD OVERLAY = GOD'S PURITY

Both the inside and outside of the Ark, however, were overlaid with pure gold. *Gold symbolizes purity* throughout the Bible. For gold to be purified, it must be heated at a high temperature until it melts. Then the alloys and impurities are skimmed off. Revelation 3:18 speaks of gold "tried in the fire."

We, too, undergo God's purification process. As we are refined and purified, we are better able to reflect the nature of God. Although we are human, we can allow God to forge us in the fires of his Spirit and to overlay our lives with purity for others to see.

As you allow God to cover you with himself, your fleshly, earthly life will no longer show through. You will become covered completely by the glory of God, and you will be required to live within the bounds of that glory. This is not always the easy way to live, but it's the *best* way! Our words, actions, and associations are subject to eternal purification.

GOLD OUTSIDE = LIFE SEEN

It is of no use simply to have *gold on the outside,* however. Jesus rebuked the Pharisees and called them hypocrites for doing just that. He said in Matthew 23:25, ". . . for ye make clean the outside of the cup and of the platter, but within they are full of extortion and excess."

GOLD INSIDE = UNSEEN LIFE

How do we become overlaid *in and out with purity?* Well, to begin, we need to recognize that God and God alone is the one who overlays our inner lives with gold. We cannot do that ourselves. What we *can* do is recognize our need for purity. We don't care about being washed until we feel unclean. That's one of the best reasons I know to read the Bible. There we have a mirror that reveals our unclean nature to us. The Scriptures show us attitudes in our lives that are displeasing to God. As we become aware of our displeasing natures, we go to God in repentance (turning from the things that are displeasing to God). Through his forgiveness and cleansing of our lives, we become purer. The impurities in our thoughts, feelings, motives, and attitudes are skimmed off through repentance, forgiveness, and a change of heart.

As God, through the Holy Spirit, shows you things in your life that need to be purified, say to him, "I give you permission, Lord, not only to put your glory on the outside of my life, but to put your glory within." This involves true surrender to God.

To be purified does not mean that you give up your individual personality or your talents. Gold overlay always takes the basic shape of whatever structure it covers. "He knoweth our frame; He remembereth that we are dust" (Psalm 103:14). God will use your basic personality, talents, education, and experiences as the basic structure. Purification *does* mean that God's priorities become yours. You are now held responsible for a bright, pure testimony for God. It also means that you no longer need to defend yourself. He is your covering and defender. Don't got your fingerprints on God's glory!

CROWN = INHERITANCE

Next we see that God ordered a crown to be placed around the top of the Ark. The crown represents victory. It also represents royalty. We, too, have a crown, an *inheritance that Jesus left us.*

Revelation 3:11 says, "Behold, I come quickly: hold that fast which thou hast, that no man take thy crown." Jesus won a crown for us by being victorious in life, death, and resurrection. He has left us a wreath of victory over death and over the devil. We are children of a King, and we share in his royalty.

Just as a royal child *anticipates* and prepares for being a monarch someday, we anticipate the promise of the crown. We live now like a royal child, confident in the power and riches we will someday have, and aware of the authority and responsibility this crown represents. We need to begin to learn how to rule and reign as God's children on earth, because we will someday inherit the earth and be responsible for it.

GOLDEN RINGS = GOD'S LOVE

God ordered golden rings placed on the four corners of the Ark. These were used to hold the Ark together. All other pieces of furniture in the Tabernacle were held together by interior silver pinnings, but the Ark did not need these.

These pure golden circles are a symbol of *God's complete love* that holds his children together permanently. I believe God is bringing his people together today to make them one body with no silver pinnings. God's people are held together across denominational and cultural lines by golden love circles that will last forever. They show the outside world that the *lasting* pinning together of people happens by God's love.

STAVES = MINISTRY

Staves were placed through the golden rings to support the Ark. These staves were made of wood, a substance representing people, again overlaid with pure gold, a substance indicating God at work. I believe these staves refer to the people who are a part of great *ministries today* that cross denominational boundaries, countries, and culture. These are human beings who have been covered by the glory of God and who are privileged to bear the weight of the Ark of God. They receive no glory for themselves because they are overlaid with the testimony of God. They help bridge us together as loving members in the body of Christ.

The staves of the Ark were never to be removed from the rings, so the Ark would be ready to move at the instant God commanded it to be moved. When God moves today, he wants his people ready and united to move with him. The Bible says we are pilgrims and strangers here on earth. "For here have we no continuing city, but we seek one to come . . . whose builder and maker is God" (Hebrews 13:14; 11:10).

MERCY SEAT = JESUS' MERCY

The lid or covering of the Ark was called the mercy seat. It was made of *solid* gold—not wood overlaid with gold. Solid gold represents something directly from God. According to the New Testament, the mercy of God is shown to us through the Lord Jesus. He was not made from dust, as Adam was; his origin was from heaven. He was pure, without sin, spot, or blemish; and it is only through his mercy covering our lives that the Spirit of God dwells within us. We do not have this mercy in ourselves. *Jesus is our covering.* He alone gives us a seat of righteousness before God's eyes. Revelation 5:12 says, "Worthy is the Lamb that was slain to receive power, and riches, and wisdom, and strength, and honour, and glory, and blessing."

SEAL – HOLY SPIRIT

How is this mercy seat held on the Ark? It is *sealed.* Scripture says this *seal represents the Holy Spirit* and the gifts to be used until the Perfect One (Jesus) comes in the day of redemption. The Holy Spirit is the cohesive force that keeps the mercy seat of Jesus protecting the believers.

Paul writes in Ephesians 1:13 that ". . . ye were sealed with that holy Spirit of promise." He goes on to say in Ephesians 4:30, "And grieve not the holy Spirit of God, whereby ye are sealed unto the day of redemption."

GOLDEN CHERUBIM = TESTED ANGELS

To top off the Ark, the Lord ordered two golden cherubim on either side! These are angels God gives us for protection. Their wings were outstretched, ready for action. They represent the soft security and warmth of being covered by feathers. They were to be made of beaten gold that had been purified and tested. We, too, are *protected by "tested angels."*

When Lucifer fell from heaven, he took one-third of the angels with him. They became demons. We hear a lot about them today. But do you realize that God still has two-thirds—twice as many—of the angels on his side? They are purified, tested, proven, unfallen angels who resisted the call of Lucifer. They are at God's command today to protect us and help us in our battle against evil! We must learn to accept the existence of angels, God's servants ministering to the heirs of salvation (Hebrews 1:13, 14). We must anticipate these golden cherubim with their wings outstretched for our protection. On the Ark,

Ark of the Covenant

A Symbol of Devout Believers in the Last Generation

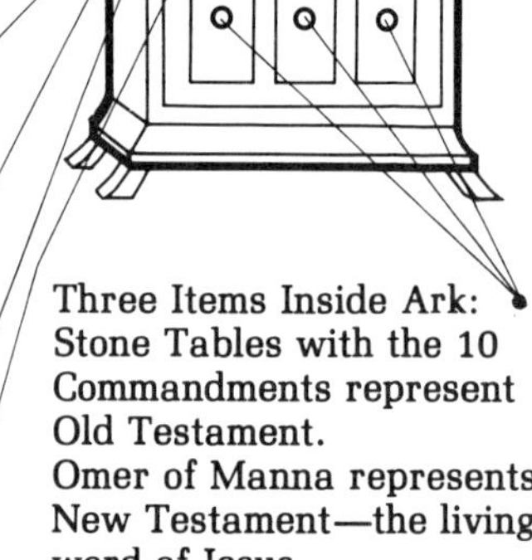

Angels—represent the guardian angels that are our protection as believers

The Mercy Seat—is our redemption through death of Jesus Christ.

Crown—represents victory and our inheritance in Jesus Christ

Seal—represents our being sealed into relationship with the Lord Jesus through the Holy Spirit.

Staves—wood overlaid with gold; represent cross-denominational ministries

Gold Rings—show God's complete love that holds his children together permanently.

Three Items Inside Ark:
Stone Tables with the 10 Commandments represent Old Testament.
Omer of Manna represents New Testament—the living word of Jesus.
Aaron's Rod that Budded represents supernatural spoken word of God's Holy Spirit.

The Ark was made of wood (representing our humanity), overlaid inside and out with pure gold (representing God's purity).

The gold inside represents our unseen life; the gold outside represents our external life—the seen life.

the angels faced the mercy seat so God could direct them to provide protection wherever battle might erupt. The angels that protect our lives are under the command of the Lord to move on our behalf in the same way.

ITEMS INSIDE THE ARK

Now let's look at three items that were placed inside the Ark. I believe these objects represent three forms of the Word of God that are to abide in each of us. Jesus said, "If ye abide in me, and my words abide in you, ye shall ask what ye will, and it shall be done unto you" (John 15:7). That is a "carte blanche" to the total power of God! God trusts us with his power when his Word abides within us.

STONE TABLES = GOD IN OLD TESTAMENT

First, there were the stone tables on which the Ten Commandments were written. (See Deuteronomy 10:1-5.) These commandments were given at Mount Sinai where the Ark was built.

The tables of stone represent the written word of God. This is the Old Testament—available for all so they may see the ways in which God has dealt with man.

MANNA = JESUS IN NEW TESTAMENT

The second object inside the Ark was manna, the food God gave freely and plentifully to his children in the wilderness, before the Ark was built. God commanded the Israelites to "Fill an omer of [manna] to be kept for your generations; that they may see the bread wherewith I have fed you in the wilderness . . ." (Exodus 16:32).

The manna represents the *Logos* or the living Word. We know that *Jesus is the Logos*, the living expression of God, and we have his words recorded in the New Testament. That is the Word on which we stand today. Just as the manna gave physical life to the Israelites, so the words of Jesus give us spiritual life.

AARON'S ROD = HOLY SPIRIT NOW

The third object inside the Ark was Aaron's rod (Numbers 17:6-10). Aaron's rod, or walking stick, was just a tree branch until God put his power into it. With renewed life the branch budded and bore fruit. God told the Israelites that Aaron's rod should "be kept for a token against the rebels."

This third form of the Word of God, and one not so commonly known, is *rhema*, the *supernatural spoken word* of God's Holy Spirit. When we speak the Word of God, the Word carries authority, brings renewed life, and bears spiritual fruit. The Scriptures say we need this supernatural spoken Word as a token against those who come against us. A very powerful example is found in Acts 5:1-5 when Peter spoke the truth of God. God will endow your words with power in *specific* instances against *specific* enemies. This is the *rhema* Word of God.

All three forms of the Word of God are to live within us, just as these objects occupied the Ark.

THE ARK IN MOTION

We are built to be the Ark of God. We have the presence of God dwelling in us and we are filled with his Word. Now we are ready for something to happen! The Ark wasn't just an object. It had a function. Let's look at the *use* or purpose of the Ark.

It is important to realize that the Ark stayed at Mount Sinai for quite a long time after it was finished. If you are under the guidance of a minister in a church as you are being formed into his special vessel, you are better off to stay under that ministry until God gets ready to move you. This is a basic principle of God. Too often when we feel a little power or glory we fly off in some direction too soon. God does not work that way. He is never in a hurry.

The Ark stayed at Sinai because God told the people they had to stay there until they stopped their murmuring and complaining and learned the lessons God wanted them to learn in order that they might become strong.

God will keep you at your Mount Sinai as long as you are murmuring and complaining about your lot in life and about God. You will stay there until you have learned his lessons and have become strong through knowing and practicing his Word.

PREPARE TO MOVE = BLOOD COVERING

When God was ready for his Ark to move, he did not send out the shiny golden Ark for all the world to see. The Ark was to be *covered with skins* when it was moved. The shedding of blood was required to provide that protection. (Compare Exodus 12:21-31.) Similarly, the blood on the doorposts had kept Israel's firstborn sons from death when the death angel stalked Egypt. God wants to protect you today in the same manner. That *protection* is provided through the *shed blood of Jesus*. If you accept the protection of Jesus, you never have to be defeated. Psalm 91:7 says, "A thousand shall fall at thy side, and ten thousand at thy right hand; but it shall not come nigh thee." Earthquakes, plane crashes, foreign governments—all manner of evil—can touch you only by God's permission. Satan's darts cannot pierce through his covering to harm the glory of God in your life.

BLUE CLOTH = HOPE OF HEAVEN

A blue cloth covered the skins (see Numbers 4:6). Blue refers to the heavens. God covers us, too, with a blanket of the heavenlies, so that people can see that *our lives are aimed at heaven*.

Have you ever heard someone say, "If ever I've seen a saint, she's one"? Or, "Goodness, I can't understand his values. The world doesn't look at things that way." We are to bear an aura of heaven about us—a covering of blue—so others will recognize us as a source of information about heaven. We are admonished to "be ready always to give an answer to every man that asketh you a reason of the hope that is in you . . ." (1 Peter 3:15).

The hope of heaven purifies us even as he is pure (1 John 3:2, 3). We are to have a "we win in the end" attitude. This hope of heaven is our testimony to the world. It's the basis for our enthusiasm as we move through the world at God's command.

MOVE ON! = FIRST OUT!

When God was ready for his people to move on into the unknown, the Ark led the way. It led the way into battles against enemies that had to be conquered. It was the first thing to leave camp. In these last years, God's children are the ones who are going to lead the way. They are to be at the front lines of spiritual battles that must be won before the Lord's return.

The first journey of the Ark was only three days. When God gives you a mission and calls you to lead and help others, he will put you out only a little at first. Jesus told his followers to be witnesses in Jerusalem—right where they were—and then to go to Judea, Samaria, and the uttermost part of the earth (Acts 1:8). That is the way God moves his vessels—first, close to home, and then farther and farther out.

ENEMY CAMP = PERSECUTION

As the Israelites fought battle after battle in order to possess the promised land, the Ark was captured and taken into an enemy camp for some time. (See 1 Samuel 4 and 5.) As we observe what is happening in the world today, we must realize that we are fighting enemies also. We may be captured as prisoners. Remember, though, that being in an enemy camp does not mean the end. God is ever-present—even in enemy camps! We must love our enemies when we are *persecuted by them.* In many parts of the world today, believers are prisoners for Jesus' sake and are suffering severe persecution (see Matthew 5:11, 12). Pray for the believers in Russia, Cambodia, Iran, and other lands.

AN UNNEEDED CART = MAN'S SYSTEMS

God made a way for the Ark to get out of the enemy camp. As the Israelites prepared to transport it back home, they decided to build a cart to carry it (see 2 Samuel 6:1-7). Normally, the Ark was carried on the shoulders of the priests as God had directed.

We need to understand that God never needs us to build an organizational vehicle for his moving or his working. He only needs strong priestly shoulders. The cart was made of wood—all of man's doing—and God was displeased with it. As God's Ark in these last days, we should not feel we *must* have an organization in order to enhance the power of God. Man's systems are *not necessary for God to work.* God can give an administrative system so simple—yet so powerful—that it boggles man's mind. We are not to build an organization and then say, "See what I've done for you, God. Bless my efforts." God's ways—not an organization or man's ways—must be uppermost in our lives. God does not need the usual rituals of the world to accomplish his work.

The Israelites realized their mistake. They had disobeyed and not operated in the way God had directed. They made a sacrifice to God, and the glory of God returned to the Ark. The Ark was carried back to Jerusalem and rested there.

You can be sure the Israelites didn't make this mistake again. It's much easier for us to obey as we move along. That keeps us moving in God's power. First Samuel 15:22 says, "Behold, to obey is better than sacrifice."

ARK LOPSIDED = UNSTEADY LEADERS

While the Ark was being moved by the cart, it was shaken as the oxen pulled it. A man tried to steady the Ark with his hand (see 2 Samuel 6:2-7). God was displeased, and the man died for touching the Ark. God alone provided total protection for the Ark. He does the same for us! With his protection, what else and whom else do we need?

The converse is also true. Sometimes we see a special Christian leader who is traveling along life's roads a little lopsided. God may be moving that person from one place to another in his or her ministry. As the person tries to follow the direction of the Holy Spirit he may appear a little unsteady. But God is the one who should steady that individual. It is not our responsibility. Don't lay a hand on God's anointed (1 Chronicles 16:22). Pray for that unsteady "ark." Pray that he or she will find the right direction in God.

VICTORY ROUTE

The Ark led the way into battle . . . and won the war!

It held back the waters of the Jordan River while the Israelites crossed over on dry soil to inherit a new and *promised land.*

Scripture tells us in Revelation 11:19, "And the temple of God was opened in heaven, and there was seen in *his temple the ark of his testament*. . . ." We, too, will have our final resting place in God's eternal place of worship—heaven—and we will dwell there forever and ever. Amen! Amen!

The Ark is only one of many symbolic objects with an eternal message. I encourage you to search out others in the Bible and to apply their meanings to your life.

Here are only three suggestions:

Noah's ark—Genesis 6 (Hint: The ark had three stories—animals on the lower deck, people on the middle deck, and a window toward heaven. See the ark as a person.)
Nehemiah's wall—Nehemiah 2 and 3 (Hint: The wall is the invisible presence of the Holy Spirit that protects us.)
Daniel's den of lions—Daniel 6 (Hint: Lions = evil beings under the authority of the Antichrist.)

Just as archaeological digs have unearthed the historical accuracy of the Bible and established it as a foundation for our faith, so symbolic "digs" can unearth the spiritual wealth of the Bible and reveal its application to our lives today.

As you start in your own study of symbols, I encourage you to do these things:

Ask the Holy Spirit to make the meanings of the symbols known to you. We must rely on the Holy Spirit to reveal the meaning of the symbols to us.

And we can be assured that as we look to the Holy Spirit for that illumination, he will be faithful to his promise to make the Word of God known to us.

Check and cross-check your interpretation of a symbol to make certain that your interpretation is valid and that it carries through to each reference of the symbol in the Bible.

A symbol *must have a* consistent meaning throughout the Bible. *It must "hold up" in all references.*

A symbol does not mean one thing in one place and another thing in another place. A symbol must carry the same meaning in every reference in the Bible for the meaning to be valid. If it does not, you have given the symbol an incorrect interpretation—however nice your idea! You must open yourself anew to an understanding by the Holy Spirit.

God is a God of order. His truth does not waver. Certainly his use of symbols is not going to become disorderly from book to book and century to century.

And finally, check your interpretation of the symbol with Bible scholars.

The symbols of the Bible are just waiting for you to unearth them . . . and apply them to your life!

VICTORIES AHEAD!

You have a fabulous life ahead as you come to know God's Word and put it to work.

I believe the conclusion of this book is really only a beginning for you in your studying the Bible for yourself. This is the place for a victory shout!

When you're in deep communication with God—the Holy Spirit stirring eternal truths in your life that cannot be adequately put into any language—you will experience the greatest sense of personal victory of your life. You will be, and *feel,* linked with Almighty God for all eternity. You will have a glimpse of divine purpose in every activity of your days, no matter how mundane. There's really no way to explain the grandeur of this experience. Your life will be at the cutting edge of spiritual awareness and of understanding world events, personal relationships, and individual needs.

The more you know the Bible, the more you pray for God's guidance in your life and involve yourself in giving to others, the more God will entrust to you.

It's time to do battle for him on the front lines of spiritual warfare. Your prayers will have no geographic limitations—you will fight spiritual battles both in your neighborhood and around the world. The more you become a friend of God, the more you become an enemy of Satan.

You'll be earning a place on Satan's "most wanted" list.

The greatest battle of Satan against you in your life will be to keep you from the Bible. A believer separated from the Bible is like a soldier separated from his sword. This, then, is the place for some *DO'S* that will keep you strong in the Lord.

DO make Bible reading the first priority of every day. Avoid the temptation of skipping a day, feeling yourself too busy or not in need of spiritual nourishment. If, however, you miss a day, *do* begin again! Don't wait until the weekend or make it next year's New Year's resolution. No matter how many days you may miss, avoid feeling guilty. Begin anew!

DO fill your home with prayer. Praise the Lord and sing songs to the Lord as you walk through your house each day. I encourage you to fill your home with beautiful God-pleasing music in the same way. You can create a truly holy atmosphere for yourself and your family. Do this for your vacation home, your car, your yard. Make the name of Jesus *present* in your life. Recognize that evil beings cannot tolerate the name of Jesus or praises to his glory!

DO rely totally on the Holy Spirit for guidance. Do turn to the Holy Spirit for confirmation of the messages you experience as you read the Bible. Do consult mature Spirit-filled friends when you have questions about the Bible. Avoid reasoning your way into an understanding of a passage apart from the illumination of the Holy Spirit!

DO take responsibility for your own mind. Our minds are ours to discipline, and discipline is a key to Bible study. We are responsible before God to be in control of our own minds and bodies. Take charge!

DO strive for balance in your Bible study. The Bible can be likened to a spiritual banquet table—an ever-available feast for your spiritual nourishment. The Bible contains all types of food—meat to chew on, sweet goodness, refreshing fruit, high-carbohydrate energy-yielding foods. All of the foods are delicious, but keeping the diet balanced requires decision and an act of your will. Many people find themselves dwelling at only one place at the table. They may concentrate their study on praise, faith, deliverance, prophecy, community, healing . . . all of which are worthy areas. But don't stop with one perspective. Study a subject, learn it, digest it, and move on. A steady diet of the same food will bore you. In fact, it can lead to malnutrition.

DO be encouraged by the examples of others who have found new life through Bible study and the love of Jesus.

Melinda, a dear friend, began a search for "reality" after the death of her father. She studied most of the religions and experiences of the world, but not the Bible. After her second visit to our Bible study group, she had an overwhelming awareness that the Bible contained what she termed the "true reality" and she invited Jesus to be her personal Lord. Immediately she began to read in Matthew as we suggested. Within a week she was doing word studies on areas that interested her, and within a month these had expanded to subject studies.

The more Melinda read the Bible, the more she knew that the Bible held the answers for her life. She discarded from her home library many, many books describing substitute experiences.

One of Melinda's friends had a heart problem, and Melinda felt such empathy with her that it seemed her own heart was breaking. She turned to the Bible for a study on "heart" and soon became involved in a series of studies that dealt with the symbolism of the heart and blood and eventually to a study of the sacrifices described in the Bible and the symbolism of the Tabernacle. Two years after she met Jesus and began reading the Bible, she is now teaching a series of Bible studies at a local church.

Because Melinda was new to our neighborhood when she began her Bible study, she and her family had few friends. She opened her home to her Bible study friends one Sunday and as she tells it now, "the party came in the door." She and her husband had never seen such abundance of food and so many children, or had ever experienced such fun. Her husband was amazed at the expression of love from those who loved the Lord and talked about the Bible with great interest. He, too, made a decision to make Jesus the Lord of his life. Throughout that year, Melinda and her husband held weekly Bible-study-and-potluck-dinners in their home. The dinners were for entire families and for persons at every level of spiritual growth—a great climate for further growing and sharing among the members of that neighborhood.

In the last two years, Melinda has seen her mother, her parents-in-law, and her sons all come to a close walk with the Lord. One son came to his relationship with Jesus after four years of intense involvement with a false religion. Today he is leading small Bible study groups on his college campus!

DO be excited about what God has planned for *you* to do and be during your life—and about what he has planned for *your* family and friends.

DO trust the Holy Spirit to make the Bible come alive for your family members. Know where to direct them in the Bible when they ask questions about what they should do—or should not do—in life. Suggest word studies. If you have an encouraging word for a person you love, perhaps you'll want to write out a word study for him or her. Avoid becoming a walking rule book or an advice column, however. Let the Holy Spirit do the guiding through the Bible.

DO use any other method of Bible study that works for you!

DO be open to receiving Bible teaching from qualified persons. God is not boxed into any one person's interpretation. Remain teachable and pliable in his hands. For example, you may encounter persons who interpret Ruth, the Psalms, or the Ark of the Covenant in different ways. Be open to receiving the added insight of others as they teach under the direction of the Holy Spirit. Avoid concluding that you have the absolute corner on God's truth. Our understanding of the truth must be constantly *enlarged,* not reduced.

DO be aware that *every* word in the Bible has meaning. Every sentence has been placed there for a purpose. The Bible was divinely inspired by the Holy Spirit. He didn't waste a single word or use any word ill-advisedly.

DO open your life to accept the truth, act upon the truth, and give the truth to others!

DO remember that legions of highly organized angels are standing ready to help you win spiritual battles at the command of God. You have a host of help on your side!

DO remember that Satan is a defeated foe. He has already lost the ultimate battle. The book of Revelation says so! We will win in the end!

DO look forward with great anticipation to the "prize of the high calling of God in Christ Jesus" (Philippians 3:14). Do look ahead with joy to the day when Jesus will return to earth to establish his reign forever.

In that day, you and I will be able to share with each other what the Bible has meant to our lives—the health and help it has been to us and how it has been very life to our bones. We will be able to share the joys together in that glorious day the Lord has planned for us, when . . .

. . . all knowledge will be revealed and we will understand all of the Word of God with a perfect understanding (1 Corinthians 13:12).

. . . all suffering will cease.

. . . we will know no more pain, emotional hurts, tears, fears, or darkness.

. . . no barriers will stop us—no walls, no mathematical formulas, no spiritual blocks will keep us from moving about the universe with total freedom.

. . . the roses will be without thorns.

. . . we will be free of the curse of competition, the process of aging, etc. All pressures and tensions of making a living that tug at us in our lives today will be gone.

. . . all necessities of life will bo met for us.

. . . little children will lead a lion and a lamb on a leash together.

. . . we will be able to know the minds of one another in a perfect sense of communication.

. . . we will be able to perceive situations and meanings accurately.

. . . we will be useful, much needed, and no secrets will be kept from us.

. . . *we will be whole, complete beings.*
. . . *we will dwell in the light of the glory of the Lord—his glory will be our very existence!*

You and I as believers and the Bible will last for all eternity, forever and ever in the presence of Almighty God, world without end! This will be the victory of victories. What a glory that will be—forever whole, together, and united in God's love!

See you then!

Bobi